The Kate Venter
Sugar Art Collection

MEREHURST

Published 1993 by Merehurst Limited
Ferry House, 51/57 Lacy Road, Putney, London, SW15 1PR
By arrangement with Tafelberg Publishers Ltd
First edition 1993

© 1993 Tafelberg Publishers Ltd

ISBN 1-85391-140-2

A catalogue record for this book is available
from the British Library.

The Kate Venter Sugar Art Collection is a compilation of
selected material that appeared in *Sugar Art, Sugar Decorating*
and *Say it with Sugar*.
Photography by Tony Abegglen and Dick Bomford
Illustrations by Janet Walker, Alice Howard and Anne Westoby
Cover and typography by G&G Design
Set in 10 on 12 pt Monotype Lasercomp Plantin
Printed and bound by
Toppan Printing Company (H.K.) Ltd, Hong Kong

I dedicate this book to my students,
whose devotion to our craft has been an inspiration

Contents

Basic equipment and aids 9
The icing bag (9) Icing tubes (10) Baking tins (10) Turntable (11) Modelling tools (11) Mixing bowls (11) Knives (11) Brushes (11) Chalk (11) Rulers (11) Rose nail (11) Florist's tape (11) Wire cutter (12) Cutters (12) Work board (12) Tweezers (12) Stamens (12) Pastry cutters (12) Florist's wire (12) Scissors (12) Rolling-pins (12) Muslin cloth (12) Colouring (12) Gum powder (12) Polystyrene (12) Table tennis balls or marbles (12) Sugar thermometer (12)

Recipes 13
Rich fruit cake (13) Light fruit cake (14) Balance in tiered cakes (14) Butter icing (14) Glacé icing and marbling (14) Almond paste or marzipan (15) Uncooked almond paste (15) Cooked almond paste (15) How to cover a cake with almond paste (15) Uncooked fondant or plastic icing (16) Cooked fondant or plastic icing (16) Royal icing (16) Flood icing (17) Modelling or flower paste (18) Pastillage (20) Pollen (20)

Icing methods and techniques 21

Bas-relief work 21

Flood work 21
Swan (21) Angels or cherubs (22) Little fisherman (23)

Modelling and dressing figures 24

Moulds 25
Plaster of Paris mould (25) Ceramic clay or putty mould (25)

Crimping 26

Filigree and lacework 26
Recipe for royal icing for filigree and bridge work (26) Guidelines (27) Using wax paper (28) Using plastic (28)

Built-up line work 28

Hollow line work 29

Extension and bridge work 29

Collars 31

Miscellaneous decorations 32
Lacework (32) Borders and embroidery (32) Paste ribbon (32) Glaze (32) Sugar rocks (32) Glitter (32) Rice-paper painting (33) Cocoa painting (33)

Flowers, ferns and fillers 34

Royal-icing flowers 34
Forget-me-nots (34) Rosebuds (34) Blossoms (34) Small daisy (35) Larger daisies (35)

Paste flowers 35
Anonymous flower (35) Blossoms (36) Apple blossom (36) Mock orange (36) Jasmine (36) Hyacinth (37) Daisy (37) Sweetpea (37) Carnation (38) Frangipani (38) Open rose (39) Cécile Brunner rose (39) Tea rose (40) Cymbidium (42) Poorman's orchid (43) Moth orchid (44) Agapanthus (45) Peruvian lily (47) Azalea (49) Baby's breath (50) Broom (51) Flame-lily (52) Fuchsia (54) Honeysuckle (56) Lilac (57) Maidenhair fern (57) Nasturtium (58) Tiger lily (60) Forget-me-not (62) Purple wreath (62) Chrysanthemum (64) Double gypsophila (66) Cattleya orchid (67) Bank's rose (70) Camel's foot (71) Blushing bride (73) Wallflower (76) China flower (76) Wild iris (77) Cosmos (79)

Cakes for special occasions 81

Patterns 124

Edges and embroidery 159

Extra embroidery patterns 162

Patterns for lacework 169

Alphabets and figures 172

Patterns for cake with pastillage decorations 176

Basic equipment and aids

A collection of basic equipment (see *plate 1*) is an essential investment for the serious cake deco- rator. You can build this up gradually as you progress in sugar art.

The icing bag

Bags made of material are on the market, but make your own out of greaseproof paper as these are easier to handle and more hygienic.

Cut out a rectangle of 230 mm × 350 mm (9⅛ in. × 14 in.) from a piece of greaseproof paper (refer to first diagram on *fig. 1*). Fold over diag- onally so that a and b on the second diagram are of equal length. Number the points as indicated on the third diagram. Lay down flat with point 1 on your left and the short side running parallel to the table. Fold the paper over to the right and flatten to form point 4. Unfold again.

Press point 4 firmly onto the table with the right-hand thumb and turn point 1 in with the left hand as indicated on the fifth diagram of *fig. 1*. Grip points 1 and 3 firmly.

Now fold point 2 over with the right hand from right to left around the front to bring it in line with point 3 at the back. Pull tight and grip firmly to form point 4. Pin 1, 3 and 2 together on the outside with a sterilised pin. Cut away point 4 to form an opening of 15 mm (⅝ in.) (see last diagram), or adjust this size to the corresponding icing pipe.

Insert the tube into the cut point, fill the bag

Plate 1
Basic equipment for sugar art

9

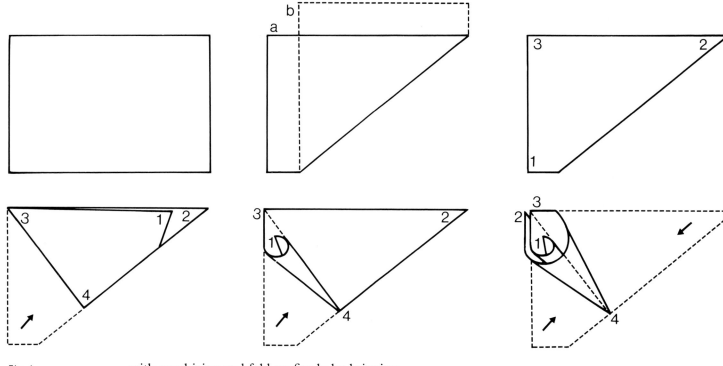

Fig. 1
How to fold the icing bag

with royal icing and fold up firmly by bringing the highest point at the back forward, folding the two sides inwards and then rolling up the top end to the front.

Icing tubes

For embroidery, writing and lace work, as well as for the formation of dots and lines, *writing tubes* in six different sizes are necessary. These are Nos. 000, 00, 0, 1, 2 and 3.

Star tubes, which are serrated at the narrow end, vary in numerical size according to make. With the Tala tube as basis for comparison, a set of three, Nos. 5, 7 and 13, will be enough for the beginner.

For piping blossoms, little roses, lace, frills, ribbons and so on, *petal* and *leaf tubes* are necessary. They are on the market, and like the star tubes, vary in numerical size according to make. Home-made bags can be substituted for leaf tubes: fold a bag according to *fig. 1* but only as far as the sixth diagram – do not cut away the sharp tip of the cone. Fill the bag with royal icing up to the tip. Fold the top end up as described in the last paragraph under *The icing bag*.

Flatten the tip (see first diagram of *fig 2*), cut across (5 mm [¼ in.] above the tip) and cut an inverted V about 2 mm (1/16 in.) deep in the middle of it. Make 3 mm (⅛ in.) diagonal cuts on either side of the legs of the V to form a W (see last diagram of *fig. 2*).

To form a leaf, place the point of the tube on a board. Press the bag and simultaneously lift your hand. Gradually decrease the pressure to let the leaf end in a sharp point. The greater the pressure the larger the leaf, and vice versa.

The W in the size given above is a good average to practise with. Work on a board at first and allow the piped leaves to dry and harden. You can work directly onto a cake at a later stage when you have acquired the necessary confidence. The size of the W can then also be adjusted accordingly.

In order to form a very small leaf, follow a different procedure when cutting the bag. Do not make a horizontal cut above the tip, but two diagonal cuts of 3 mm (⅛ in.) each that will cross each other in the middle to form a V (see *fig. 3*).

Baking tins

Standard round or square cakes are baked in 300 mm (12 in.), 200 mm (8 in.) and 150 mm (6 in.) tins. When you bake a fruit cake, line the tin or tins as follows:

Measure the circumference and the height of the tin, then, adding 20 mm (¾ in.) for the length and 20 mm (¾ in.) for the width, cut out two cor-

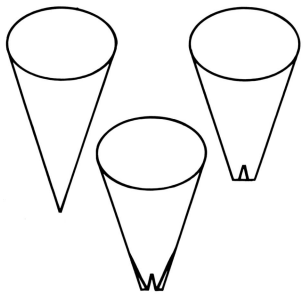

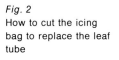

Fig. 2
How to cut the icing bag to replace the leaf tube

Mixing bowls

Plastic bowls should not be used for mixing as they contain a certain amount of grease. Use earthenware, glass or stainless-steel bowls.

Knives

Three sets of knives will be enough for the beginner: a small spatula or spreader for mixing and spreading royal icing; a palette knife or artist's spatula with a blade of about 20 mm × 110 mm ($\frac{3}{4}$ in. × $4\frac{3}{8}$ in.) for lifting and handling small petals, leaves, lacework, figures, etc.; and a scalpel for cutting out designs and making small or fine cuts.

Brushes

About five round artist's brushes (Nos. 00, 0, 1, 2 and 3) are necessary for flood work and for painting flowers and other motifs. A No. 6 round brush for dusting flowers with chalk is also recommended. Invest in two flat-tipped brushes (Nos. 10 and 1 respectively) for rice-paper painting.

Chalk

Edible chalk is used in dry form to colour and give depth to designs and flowers. A wide variety of tints and shades can be obtained by mixing white and the three basic colours (red, blue and yellow). Colours can be lightened with cornstarch instead of white chalk. A wide range of commercial colours is also available.

Rulers

In addition to an ordinary ruler, a handy set of four circular dividers is available for marking cakes into various sections.

Rose nail

This consists of a metal nail for easy handling and a flat top of about 25 mm (1 in.) to 30 mm ($1\frac{1}{4}$ in.) in diameter to serve as a base on which to make flowers from royal icing. A practical rose nail can be made by using a bottle top stuck onto the head of a long and fairly thin nail.

Florist's tape

A self-adhesive tape is available in different colours. A special cutter, as shown in *plate 1*, is a very useful device for cutting the tape into even halves, thirds or quarters. Green tape is used for covering florist's wire to make stems for flowers, leaves and so on.

Florist's ribbon, available in standard widths, is used together with flowers for a more delicate look in arrangements. It can also be divided with a tape cutter.

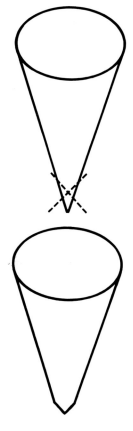

Fig. 3
How to cut the icing bag to pipe very small leaves

responding rectangles from brown paper and one from greaseproof paper. These are used to line the inside of the tin. Fold 20 mm ($\frac{3}{4}$ in.) back along one of the lengths and unfold again. Make cuts up to the crease all along this 20 mm ($\frac{3}{4}$ in.) strip. Grease the tin well and position the first piece of brown paper around the inside so that the fringed strip will lie on the bottom. Press the paper firmly against the side of the tin. Grease with butter or margarine, then repeat the whole procedure with the second piece of brown paper and the greaseproof paper.

Now cut two pieces of brown and one of greaseproof paper to fit the bottom of the tin. Line as for the sides.

Do *not* grease the last layer as the shortening in the recipe on page 13 will prevent the cake from sticking to it.

Finally tie four layers of newspaper around the tin. This ensures that an even temperature will spread through the cake from the outside to the inside, which will result in a cake with a flat, not a rounded surface.

Turntable

This can be made of wood (as in *plate 1*) or of stainless steel. It is not essential, as a cake or biscuit tin can be used instead, but it does make matters easier.

Modelling tools

Wooden or plastic tools are available in sets and are essential for modelling leaves, petals and miscellaneous figures. Pewter tools can be used instead if you like. Marzipan and plastic icing or flower paste are mainly used for modelling work.

Wire cutter

This should be very sharp and of good quality so that the wire stems of flowers can be cut neatly into required lengths.

Cutters

These are used for pressing out shapes such as keys, numbers, letters, petals, leaves and other figures of flower paste or plastic icing.

Work board

This serves as a general work surface. I find that a 250 mm × 300 mm (10 in. × 12 in.) board is a useful size and prefer a wooden board covered with self-adhesive plastic in a pastel chequered design.

Tweezers

These are indispensable for delicate work. A standard pair and a long pair with a curved point should form part of your basic equipment.

Stamens

These can be found in different colours in hobby and craft shops. White and yellow are mainly used, and the finer they are, the more delicate the work. You can also manage quite well with white only if you use colouring to dye this for your requirements.

Pastry cutters

Three kinds are necessary: a pastry cutter for cutting designs out of plastic icing or flower paste; a dressmaker's tracing wheel to copy a design onto a cake and to finish off paste ribbons, imitate stitching and so on; and a parsley cutter for cutting plastic icing or flower paste into even strips for ribbons.

Florist's wire

This is obtainable in different gauges and is used mainly for flower stems. I usually keep Nos. 18, 20, 22, 24 and 26 in stock.

Scissors

Two pairs are necessary: an ordinary pair for cutting out paper patterns and a small pair with long, sharp blades for making flowers out of flower paste.

Rolling-pins

Different sizes are used for rolling out marzipan, plastic icing and flower paste. A small one for flower paste can be made out of a piece of chrome tubing or towel rail (about 18 mm ($\frac{3}{4}$ in.) in diameter and 150 mm (6 in.) in length).

Muslin cloth

Cover royal icing with a damp muslin cloth to prevent it from forming a crust. Strain the white of an egg through a piece of dry cloth to prevent threads of egg white from breaking up in the icing. Shape a piece of dry cloth into a pad and use it to smooth marzipan or plastic icing.

Colouring

Vegetable colouring is available in liquid, powder and paste form, all of which are used for the same purpose.

Gum powder

Mix gum powder into plastic icing to make flower paste with a more pliable consistency. Three kinds are available: gum tragacanth which is very expensive, and carboxy methyl cellulose or CMC or Tylose C 1000 P, which also results in a whiter flower paste.

Polystyrene

The stems of completed flowers may be stuck into blocks of polystyrene for drying and storage, and modelled petals or leaves can be placed in individual cups of polystyrene fruit containers for shaping and drying.

Table tennis balls or marbles

These are used for drying shaped petals and other rounded designs (see *plate 18*).

Sugar thermometer

Essential for preparing plastic icing and making sugar rocks (see page 32).

Recipes

Firm cakes such as fruit cakes and Madeira cakes, which can be covered with marzipan and fondant, are mainly used for the delicate art of cake decorating as they keep for a long time. Sponge and butter cakes are too light for this method. The following recipe has been used for the past 25 years or more and is most reliable. For those who would like a rich light fruit cake I provide an alternative recipe. *Note:* Use either the metric or the imperial measurements and not a combination of the two systems.

Rich fruit cake

400 g (14 oz) raisins
400 g (14 oz) currants
400 g (14 oz) sultanas
400 g (14 oz) cherries
60 g (2 oz) glacé ginger, chopped
60 g (2 oz) fig preserve, chopped
60 g (2 oz) watermelon preserve, chopped
60 g (2 oz) glacé pineapple, chopped
275 g (10 oz) dates, chopped
175 g (6 oz) mixed peel
125 ml ($\frac{1}{2}$ cup) brandy
450 g (1 lb) cake flour
2,5 ml ($\frac{1}{2}$ t) salt
10 ml (2 t) ground cinnamon
10 ml (2 t) ground mixed spice
5 ml (1 t) ground nutmeg
5 ml (1 t) ground ginger
5 ml (1 t) baking powder
2,5 ml ($\frac{1}{2}$ t) mace
2,5 ml ($\frac{1}{2}$ t) ground cloves
350 g (12 oz) butter
350 g (12 oz) yellow sugar
8 eggs
2,5 ml ($\frac{1}{2}$ t) bicarbonate of soda, dissolved in
   15 ml (1 T) strong black coffee
15 ml (1 T) vanilla essence
8 ml ($1\frac{1}{2}$ t) almond essence
125 ml ($\frac{1}{2}$ cup) Van der Hum

Wash raisins, currants, sultanas and cherries thoroughly and leave to dry. If the rest of the fruit is very syrupy or sugary, wash and dry thoroughly as well. Mix all the fruit together in a large mixing bowl, and pour over the brandy.

Line the pans with two layers of brown and one layer of greaseproof paper, and tie a few layers of newspaper around the outside. (Refer to the instructions on page 11.) Sift all the dry ingredients together, except the bicarbonate of soda.

Cream butter and sugar, and beat in three eggs, one by one. Fold in a little of the sifted dry ingredients after the third egg.

Sprinkle two handfuls of dry ingredients over the fruit mixture and mix well.

Mix the rest of the dry ingredients and the remaining five eggs alternately into the butter mixture. Mix well. Add the bicarbonate of soda dissolved in the coffee, as well as the two flavourings. Mix well. Add to the fruit and mix thoroughly.

Spoon into the prepared tins and bake for about $3\frac{1}{2}$ hours as follows: 1 hour at 180 °C (350 °F), 1 hour at 150 °C (300 °F), 1 hour at 130 °C (250 °F) and 30 minutes at 100 °C (200 °F).

An alternative method is to bake overnight. First bake the cake for 30 minutes at 150 °C (300 °F), then for 30 minutes at 130 °C (250 °F), then for about six hours at 100 °C (200 °F). The full baking time, therefore, is about seven hours.

Remove from the oven and pour Van der Hum over the cakes. Allow to cool in the tins.

This mixture yields one round cake of 250 mm (10 in.) in diameter or two round cakes of 200 mm (8 in.) in diameter or one square cake of 230 mm × 230 mm ($9\frac{1}{8}$ in. × $9\frac{1}{8}$ in.).

For a round cake of 300 mm (12 in.) in diameter use $1\frac{1}{2}$ times the ingredients; for a square cake of 300 mm × 300 mm (12 in. × 12 in.) use twice the ingredients; for a round cake of 350 mm (14 in.) in diameter use twice the ingredients; for a square cake of 350 mm × 350 mm (14 in. × 14 in.) use $2\frac{1}{2}$ times the ingredients; for two round cakes of 250 mm (10 in.) and 150 mm (6 in.) in diameter respectively, use $1\frac{1}{4}$ times the ingredients; and for two square cakes of 230 × 230 mm ($9\frac{1}{8}$ in. × $9\frac{1}{8}$ in.) and 150 mm × 150 mm (6 in. × 6 in.) respectively use $1\frac{1}{4}$ times the ingredients.

Light fruit cake

450 g (1 lb) whole cherries, washed and dried
350 g (12 oz) sultanas *or* 225 g (8 oz) sultanas
    and 125 g (4 oz) ginger preserve
125 g (4 oz) mixed peel
225 g (8 oz) fig preserve, washed, dried and
    chopped
225 g (8 oz) pineapple rings, drained, washed and
    chopped
225 g (8 oz) ground almonds
handful whole almonds
450 g (1 lb) cake flour
275 g (10 oz) butter
225 g (8 oz) sugar
10 ml (2 t) baking powder
pinch salt
5 large or 6 small eggs
10 ml (2 t) almond essence
80-125 ml ($\frac{1}{3}$-$\frac{1}{2}$ cup) cherry or peach liqueur

Mix the fruit and nuts in a large mixing bowl.
Sprinkle a handful of cake flour over the fruit
and mix in well.

Line a cake tin of 250 mm (10 in.) in diameter
as described on page 11.

Cream the butter and sugar.

Sift the flour, baking powder and salt together.

Add the eggs singly to the butter mixture,
beating well after each addition. Add the flour
mixture gradually, then the flavouring and fruit,
and mix well.

Bake for 3 to 3$\frac{1}{2}$ hours at 140 to 150 °C (275 to
300 °F) until done.

Remove from the oven and pour over the
liqueur immediately.

Allow to cool in the tin.

Note: This cake burns very easily. Test it after
about 2$\frac{1}{2}$ hours.

Balance in tiered cakes

Good proportions for a three-tiered cake are
round tins with a diameter of 300 mm (12 in.),
200 mm (8 in.) and 150 mm (6 in.) respectively,
or 350 mm (14 in.), 250 mm (10 in.) and 180 mm
(7 in.). Dimensions of square cakes must be in
the same proportion. The diameter of the cake
drums for the largest cake should be about
400 mm (16 in.), then 250 mm (10 in.) and 190
mm (7$\frac{1}{2}$ in.) for the two smaller cakes.

When the cakes are arranged on dividers on
top of one another a ruler positioned against the
side of all three cakes should touch the upper
edge of each cake (see arrows on *fig. 4*).

There must also be a difference of at least
12 mm ($\frac{1}{2}$ in.) in the height of the three cakes,
with the highest layer at the bottom. So if the
largest cake, which will carry the heaviest decorations, is about 90 mm (3$\frac{1}{2}$ in.) high, the middle
cake should be 78 mm (3 in.) and the top one 66
mm (2$\frac{1}{2}$ in.)

Butter icing

125 g (4 oz) butter or margarine
500 g (1 lb) icing sugar
water, milk, cream, fruit juice or other liquid
5 ml (1 t) flavouring
pinch salt
colouring (optional)

Beat the butter and add the icing sugar gradually,
beating well after each addition, until creamy. If
the mixture is too thick, add enough warm liquid
to obtain a soft and creamy mixture. Cold liquid
will cause the mixture to curdle.

Add the flavouring and salt when well mixed.
Colour if desired.

Add the white or the yolk of an egg for a
richer and less creamy consistency, but use 30 g
(1 oz) less butter.

Glacé icing and marbling

Glacé icing is cheap and can be made in minutes.
The only two ingredients are icing sugar and any
liquid at room temperature: water, orange juice
or any other fruit juice. Colour if necessary.

Combine icing sugar and liquid, and mix
quickly to form a consistency that will spread
over the cake without running off it. Work quickly as a crust forms rapidly.

You can't make decorations with this icing, but

Fig. 4
How to obtain balance
for a tiered cake

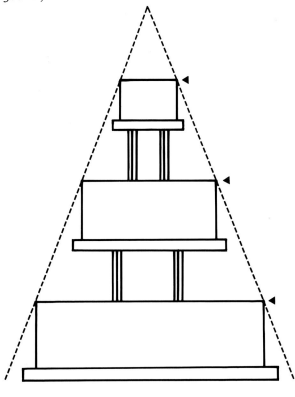

14

the mixture. If the icing mixture is too soft, the peak will curl back. If too much icing sugar has been used, the peak will break off bluntly.

If too stiff, dip a spatula with a small quantity of icing mixture on it into beaten egg white and mix this into the rest of the icing mixture. Repeat this process until the correct consistency is reached. This method will prevent you from ending up with an enormous bowl of mixed icing.

Royal icing will be snow white if it has been mixed correctly. To make it even brighter, dip the tip of the handle of a brush into blue colouring and mix this trace into the icing. If not well mixed, it will be slightly cream in clour.

Flood icing

Flood icing has a runny consistency but is not as liquid as water. The first step is to mix a quantity of royal icing (described above). Cover with a damp muslin cloth.

The next step is to thin down small quantities of royal icing with cold water or egg white to flood a pattern in relief. (For examples of this type of work, see *plates 4 to 6*.) It is not possible to give exact proportions of the ingredients as the individual pieces of a design filled with different colours of flood icing will differ in size and shape. However, there is a test to determine approximately how much icing should be thinned for a specific area.

Use a small quantity of mixed royal icing and thin down in a separate bowl. Draw a line through the icing with the sharp edge of a knife. The consistency will be correct if the line does not close up before the count of seven. This measure is used in warm, dry weather. In cold and/or wet conditions the mixture may be slightly thicker and a count of 10 is used for the test.

To work out how much flood icing to colour for a specific area of a pattern, pour a spoonful of the mixture onto a wax-covered board. Leave to spread and set. You can then work out how many spoonfuls to prepare. Remember that it is better to mix a little more than you need, as it is virtually impossible to repeat a tint or shade.

Trace the pattern for a specific cake onto greaseproof paper down to the finest detail. Never use the original pattern to work on as parts of the design will be covered with flood icing as work begins, which will make it necessary to refer to the original design.

After tracing the pattern, place it on a flat surface such as a piece of glass, wooden board or cake drum, and secure with either Sellotape or drawing pins. The work board should be light and easy to handle.

Next, place a sheet of wax paper or thin plastic over the greaseproof paper and secure carefully. If the design moves during the flooding process, the surface will crack and look unsightly. An alternative method is to place the greaseproof paper with the design underneath a sheet of glass and secure firmly. Wash or clean, and spread the top of the glass with a small amount of vegetable fat before you begin to work.

Study the pattern intensively. Where you wish certain sections to be flooded separately for a three-dimensional effect, such as the arm from the side view of the little fisherman (see *plate 6*), trace them and place under wax paper or thin plastic on a separate board or under glass.

Decide which section on the picture is furthest in perspective from the viewer, and mark it No. 1. Number each individual section from No. 2 upwards moving towards the viewer. When the flood work begins, the picture is built up in dimensions by working gradually from the back to the front, that is, starting with No. 1 and ending with the highest number.

The next step is to colour enough royal icing in separate bowls for the different sections of the picture. Please note that best results for dark colours are obtained by using dry undiluted powdered colouring.

Divide each colour between two bowls. The one quantity remains as it is, while the other is thinned down as described for flood work. Never work the other way round (first colouring the flood icing, then thickening it for the piping) as this will result in the icing for the outline being lighter than the icing for the flood work.

Start with section 1. Outline with a No. 1 writing tube and the appropriate colour in royal icing, then flood the space carefully with the corresponding colour in flood icing. (An icing bag without a tube can be used for this purpose – cut the opening to the size of a No. 1 tube.) Under no circumstances must the picture be outlined all at once as this will spoil the three-dimensional effect that you want to achieve. Do not fill the outlines with too much flood icing as it will flow onto other sections of the pattern.

Pipe flood icing into the centre of the outlined section and work this gradually up to the edges with a No. 1 round-tipped paintbrush of good quality. Paint the flood icing carefully onto the outline so that an integrated whole will be formed without the icing overflowing onto the wax paper or thin plastic.

Flood the rest of the picture in a similar fashion, according to the numbers. If No. 2, for example, is next to section No. 1, the latter should be left until completely dry before beginning the former.

Some sections will obviously overlap other sections, such as a hand on material or a bow in the hair. If this is the case, great care must be taken not to disturb the perspective. For instance, fingers can look like bananas if made too large. If the hand rests on clothing, the clothing should be flooded first. Pipe the outline of the clothing with royal icing, just inside the outlines of the hand. When this has been flooded the outline of the hand, corresponding exactly in size to the pattern, will be piped on top of the edge of the clothing, and then filled with flood icing to normal size. The hand will then automatically be higher than the clothing.

The swan in *plate 4* is a good pattern for the beginner to use for developing skills and acquiring experience.

Modelling or flower paste

As the name implies, this paste is used for moulding flowers and other decorations (see pages 34 to 80). Three recipes are given; the first is recommended for use in winter-rainfall areas or regions where the humidity is high.

Recipe 1
25 ml (5 t) cold water
10 ml (2 t) gelatine
15 ml (1 T) white vegetable fat (15 g)
800 ml (14 oz) sifted icing sugar (400 g)
25 ml (5 t) gum tragacanth or CMC
35 ml (7 t) egg white (1 large egg), strained
    through a muslin cloth and beaten until white
    and frothy

Place the 25 ml (5 t) cold water in a small bowl, sprinkle the gelatine over and allow it to sponge.

Grease a large glass bowl with some of the fat and suspend it over a saucepan of hot water (the bottom of the bowl should not touch the water). Place half the icing sugar in the bowl, add the gum tragacanth or CMC and stir. Transfer to the stove and bring the water to the boil. Leave for about 10 minutes to heat the icing sugar (take care not to overheat it).

Melt the sponged gelatine over hot water.

Remove the bowl from the saucepan. Make a well in the icing sugar and add the gelatine and beaten egg white. *Beat well until the mixture becomes white and sticky.* This is very important as the mixture would otherwise be too soft and not white enough.

Add the rest of the icing sugar and mix well. The paste will have a fairly stiff consistency.

Rub some of the remaining fat on your hands and knead the icing mixture until it is quite cold.

Form into a smooth ball. Rub fat all over the ball, place it in a plastic bag and seal it in an airtight container.

Refrigerate for at least 12 hours.

Cut walnut-sized pieces from the hard stiff modelling paste. Grease your hands with a little fat and knead the pieces of paste until soft and pliable. Repeat until all the paste has been worked in this way, gradually combining the pieces to form one big ball again.

Roll the paste into balls the size of golf balls, grease lightly, place in a plastic bag in an airtight container and freeze until required. The paste can be stored like this indefinitely.

Microwave method for recipe 1 (with kind permission from Jeanette van Niekerk)
Place half the icing sugar and all the gum tragacanth in a greased glass bowl. Microwave on full power for 50 seconds, remove from the oven and stir well. Repeat twice more.

Microwave the soaked gelatine for 16 seconds on full power, or until clear.

Follow the instructions for recipe 1.

Note
15 ml (1 T) Tylose C 1000 P may be used instead of 25 ml (5 t) gum tragacanth or CMC, but an extra 125 ml (2 oz) (60 g) icing sugar will have to be added.

Recipe 2
10 ml (2 t) gelatine powder
25 ml (5 t) cold water
900 ml (1 lb) sifted icing sugar (450 g)
15 ml (1 T) gum tragacanth, CMC or Tylose
10 ml (2 t) liquid glucose
15 ml (1 T) white vegetable fat (15 g)
45 ml (3 T) egg white (1 extra-large egg, plus
    5-10 ml (1-2 t) more)

Soak the gelatine in the cold water.

Sift half the icing sugar and all the gum tragacanth, CMC or Tylose into a well-greased glass bowl. Place over a saucepan of boililng water and heat for approximately 10 minutes, taking care not to overheat the mixture.

In the meantime, dissolve the gelatine over hot water. Add the liquid glucose and vegetable fat, and heat until melted.

Make a well in the centre of the icing sugar. Add the egg white and gelatine mixture and stir until well incorporated.

Remove the bowl from the saucepan of boiling water and beat the mixture with a wooden spoon until quite white and sticky. Insufficient beating will result in a too-soft, off-white paste.

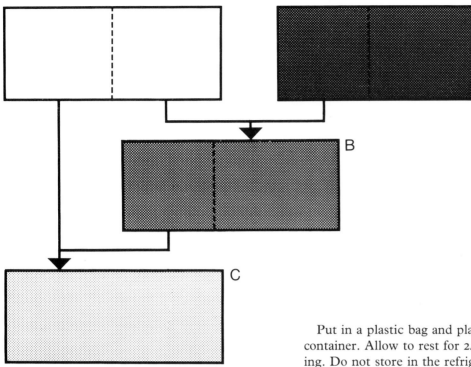

Fig. 5
How to mix modelling
paste to obtain three
tints of the same
colour

Add the rest of the icing sugar. Grease your hands with vegetable fat and knead the mixture thoroughly.

Grease the ball of paste with vegetable fat and place it in a plastic bag in an airtight container. Refrigerate for 12 to 24 hours.

See recipe 1 for the remaining kneading instructions.

Note
Do not add the glucose and fat to the gelatine before it has dissolved completely, as grey specks may otherwise form in the modelling paste.

If the paste is too hard when you want to use it, knead in small quantities of egg white or cold water to make it more pliable.

Recipe 3: Uncooked modelling paste
This recipe is mostly used during the summer months.

15 ml (3 t) gum tragacanth or CMC (see page 12)
± 500 g (1 lb) plastic icing
± 10 ml (± 2 t) egg white
± 30 g (± 1 oz) white vegetable fat

Mix the gum tragacanth into the plastic icing and knead well. The gum must be incorporated thoroughly into the paste before the egg white is added. Add the egg white, knead in the vegetable fat and knead until the paste is smooth and elastic.

Put in a plastic bag and place in an airtight container. Allow to rest for 24 hours before using. Do not store in the refrigerator.

Knead the paste very well and add more egg white if necessary.

With the correct treatment and handling this paste can keep for months. Store in a plastic bag in an airtight container in the freezer.

How to colour modelling paste
Use as much paste as will be necessary to complete all the flowers or figures that will be made from a particular colour. Remember that it is better to prepare a little more than you might need as it is virtually impossible to repeat shades and tints.

Divide the prepared white paste into two equal portions. Colour the one portion in the darkest tint that will be required and keep the other portion aside in a plastic bag.

Divide the coloured paste in two, with one portion slightly larger than the other. Put the larger portion in a plastic bag in an airtight container (call this A).

Divide the second portion of white paste in two. Put one half in a plastic bag and mix the other half with the smaller portion of the coloured paste. Knead well, then divide this lighter tint in two, again making one portion larger than the other. Keep the larger portion (call this B) in a plastic bag in an airtight container, and mix the smaller portion with the balance of the white paste for an even lighter tint (C). (See *fig. 5*.)

It is also possible to alter the contrast between the three tints by adding more white paste as desired.

Pastillage

Pastillage differs from modelling paste in that it is not moulded but rolled out and cut into shapes according to various patterns. It is used to make objects such as plaques, birthday cards, baskets, musical instruments, bells, etc. (see *plate 2*).

Recipe 1
15 ml (1 T) gelatine (10 g)
80 ml (⅓ cup) cold water
10 ml (2 t) liquid glucose
5 ml (1 t) cream of tartar, dissolved in 10 ml (2 t) cold water
500-750 ml (2-3 cups) sifted icing sugar (250-380 g)
250 ml (1 cup) cornflour (120 g)

Soak the gelatine in the cold water, then melt it over hot water.

Add the liquid glucose and cream of tartar solution. Stir until well mixed.

Place half the icing sugar and all the cornflour in a large mixing bowl. Add the liquid and beat until the mixture becomes sticky.

Pour into an airtight container and store in the refrigerator.

When needed, take the required quantity of mixture and add enough of the remaining sifted icing sugar to it to form a paste that does not stick to your hands. Roll out and cut (see *fig. 103* and *fig. 153 to 156* for examples of patterns).

Place a copy of the pattern underneath a piece of glass and secure it. Sprinkle the top of the glass with cornflour and arrange the cut-out pastillage on it to correspond with the pattern below. Leave to dry. Turn the pastillage over after several hours to allow the reverse to dry.

Repeat the turning over process several times to prevent the pieces from warping. When set, place on a piece of thick sponge to dry completely.

Recipe 2
2,5 ml (½ t) gum tragacanth
125 ml (½ cup) royal icing
sifted icing sugar

Stir the gum tragacanth into the icing, cover it with a damp cloth and, to prevent it from drying out, place it bowl and all in a plastic bag. Leave to stand overnight.

Mix well the following day, adding enough sifted icing sugar to make the pastillage very stiff. Knead well until smooth.

Use the paste for modelling animals, figures, bells, etc.

Pollen

Semolina *or* mealie-meal *or* gelatine powder
yellow colouring powder

Mix small amounts of the two ingredients together, using as much powdered colouring as necessary to obtain the tint of yellow you require.

Icing methods and techniques

Bas-relief work

This is a technique in which figures are moulded out of flower paste so that, when they are placed on a cake, they stand out slightly from the background. It can best be illustrated by means of an example (*plate 3*).

Make a photocopy of the pattern (*fig. 78*) and place it on a board. Cover it with plastic and secure it so that it cannot move.

Using the pattern as guideline, mould the flowers and leaves freehand, or use cutters of a suitable size. Set aside to dry.

Next, mould the central figure (the mouse). Start with that part of his body furthest away from you, i.e. the part of the foot visible under the stalk. Mould it freehand and place it in position. Shape the leg of this foot.

Add the trousers turn-up and tuck it under the leg with a scalpel or similar tool to create the impression that it goes all around.

Mould the hand behind the stalk and place it in position. Make the arm.

Make the flower stalk and arrange it over the hand and foot.

Mould and position the tail, second foot and trousers.

Add the second turn-up, tucking it under as well

Shape the body.

Roll out a piece of flower paste and cut out the jacket according to the pattern. Drape it over the body.

Make and position the ear furthest away from you, then shape the head and add the second ear.

Make the collar and place it in position.

Shape the second hand and arm.

Paint facial and other details on the figure.

Set aside to dry.

Make other components of the picture.

Place the photocopy of your pattern on a plaque or cake and prick out the pattern outlines with a pin or similar sharp instrument.

Paint the background and all those features not made of flower paste.

Attach the moulded parts with royal icing, starting at the focal point.

Finish off the border with roping, lace or whatever you prefer.

Plate 3
Plaque in bas-relief (see fig. 78 for pattern)

Flood work

Swan

Although the body of the swan is flat and in one solid piece, one should work carefully to capture the gracefulness of the bird.

Secure a piece of thin plastic or wax paper over the traced pattern and pipe the outlines with royal icing (see *plate 4*). Pipe the flood icing into

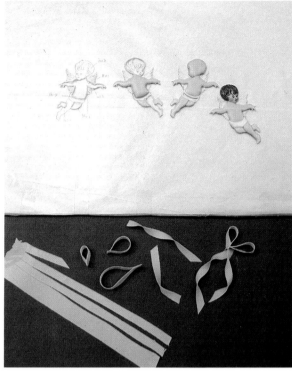

the space between the lines and use a brush to paint the icing towards and onto the outlines as described on pages 16 to 17. Start at the head and gradually fill the neck and then the body until the whole is completed.

Leave to dry thoroughly.

To lift the swan from the wax paper, remove the thumb tacks or Sellotape, hold a light flat board horizontally against the one on which the swan was made, pull the end of the wax paper through the slit between the two boards and keep on pulling until the swan has gradually moved from the one board and slipped onto the other. Or use a spatula with a very thin blade to loosen the swan from the wax paper or plastic. A length of taut cotton thread may also be inserted between the swan and the wax paper or plastic and then gradually pulled from one side to the other to loosen the swan.

Turn the swan over onto its flooded side. Do not outline again, but flood as described above. Brush the flood icing very carefully onto the outer edges, but take care that it does not overflow. When dry, the seam will be hardly visible. Put aside and make the wings.

Starting at the tip, pipe the top outline using a No. 1 writing tube with royal icing, and then pipe a series of lines close together using the same icing and tube. Use a brush to fill in any spaces between the lines. Pipe two more similar rows of lines as depicted in the photograph to form feathers and complete the main section of the wing by again piping three layers of lines in a

similar fashion. Leave to dry thoroughly and in the meantime form another wing which will be a mirror image of the first one (see *plate 4*).

Use a No. 5 star tube for assembling the different components. Pipe a pear-shaped support, push the breast of the swan into the wide end and position neatly. (*Note:* at this stage the eyes and the beak should already have been painted.) Allow to dry.

Remove the wings from the wax paper or plastic as described above, turn upside down and pipe an elongated pear shape from the rounded end towards the pointed tip using a No. 5 star tube and royal icing. Attach these wings at an angle on either side of the breast of the swan and support with small pieces of foam rubber to dry in the correct position.

Angels or cherubs

These angels (*plate 5* and *fig. 79*) are more difficult to flood than the swan as they are built up in four different stages.

A close examination of the picture reveals that the wings are situated behind the body (mark as No. 1). The one leg crosses over the other (mark them respectively Nos. 2 and 1). The head fits onto the body (mark them Nos. 3 and 2) and then finally number the loin-cloth No. 4, as this will be flooded last.

Proceed as follows:

Pipe the wings as described for the swan, using a single layer only. Start just inside the lines of the body and the arms, and work towards the outer edges of the wings. When the wings have been completed, pipe the outline of the leg marked No. 1 with flesh-coloured royal icing and a No. 1 tube. Fill in with flood icing in the same colour, as described on page 17. This leg should not be too high, otherwise the second leg, when completed, will appear to be out of proportion.

Outline the body and arms and take care to pipe the lines *over* the wings. Fill with flood icing. Then complete the second leg as follows: Pipe a short line from the foot at the back up to the loin-cloth and then from the foot down towards the ankle of the leg in front. Pipe a similar line from the already-formed thigh down towards the unformed knee. Then pipe the whole of the outline of the leg in front (over the leg at the back and the lines just completed). This prevents the leg in front from sagging unnaturally in places. Fill in with flood icing.

Pipe the outline of the head (yet again overlapping the neck of the torso) and flood. Lastly outline the loin-cloth (over the waist and legs) and flood.

Because the head of the angel is so small, components such as the hair, cheeks and nose are not built up. These are eventually completed by painting with vegetable colouring.

Hint: Always try to make more than one angel at a time to ensure that, when moving over from one numbered section to another, the previous section will be dry before the one overlapping it is flooded.

Arrange in pairs on top of or around the side of a cake and link together with garlands of flowers and/or ribbons (refer to *plate 72*).

Little fisherman

As is customary, the first step is to number the different components chronologically, working from below upwards. Here it is as follows:

1 the face, the crown of the hat, the part of the shirt underneath the sleeve, and the inside of the trousers at the back where the one brace ends;
2 the neck and back of the shirt;
3 the hair;
4 the trousers and continuous bottom brace;
5 the piece of shirt showing under the top brace and the brim of the hat;
6 the seat of the trousers above the handkerchief;
7 the top brace;
8 the left-hand part of the handkerchief;
9 the part of the handkerchief in the three-o'clock to five-o'clock position;
10 the pocket on the seat of the trousers;

Plate 6
Little fisherman

11 the piece of the handkerchief just to the left of the one mentioned under No. 9;
12 the last part of the handkerchief; and
13 the hat-band

Note: as mentioned on page 17, the little boy may be built up three-dimensionally. Therefore, trace the legs, arm and hat brim onto a separate piece of greaseproof paper (see *plate 6* and compare the complete cake on *plate 80*). Outline these and flood – in the case of the legs, first the feet and then the trouser-legs. Allow to dry.

Meanwhile, build up the face of the boy with flesh-coloured royal icing. The eyebrow-ridge, tip of the nose, cheek, lips and earlobe must be rounded and the eye-socket, ear-hole, mouth and the space between the cheek and the nose indented. Allow to dry and, if necessary, correct parts that are too rounded by sandpapering them flatter. It is also not too late to build up parts that are too flat with additional royal icing. Pipe the outline of the face and flood.

Complete the rest of the boy step by step, taking special care when forming the crown of the hat: only outline the left and right panels; then flood and allow to dry. Then pipe a blue line from panel to panel about 1 mm ($\frac{1}{25}$ in.) lower than the top line of the hat-band. Flood *without* piping lines for the middle panel. Just push the icing against the outer edge of the previous panels. In this way a natural crease will be obtained.

When completely dry, paint the face and paint

23

Fig. 6

Modelling the legs and
arms of a figure

little white dots on the shirt, sleeve, handkerchief and hat-band. Pipe white stitches along the creases of the hat with white royal icing and a No. o writing tube. Pipe the hair with a No. I writing tube. Lastly attach the brim of the hat (flooded separately) along the lower edge of the hat-band with royal icing to stand away slightly from the face. Flood the hat-band.

Assemble on the cake as depicted on *plate 80.* Roll a piece of blue fondant out thinly and cut to form a pool of water. Attach to the cake with royal icing. Make the rocks as explained on page 32 and arrange around the banks of the pool. The rock on which the little boy is sitting is made of fondant.

The individual sections of the boy are attached section by section with royal icing: first the body, then the arms and the legs. The fishing-rod made of modelling paste is then placed between the hands, with the rod extending over the hip where it is attached to the body (a clever piece of camouflage!)

Attach the tin with bait, the fish and the frog (all separately flooded), and form a fishing-line with black royal icing and a No. I writing tube. Also form tufts of reeds from vermicelli and royal icing (first colour and attach the former, and then make seed-pods with brown royal icing and a No. I writing tube).

To make sand and gravel, crush sugar rocks with a rolling-pin and press in on the foreground. Dilute royal icing with water until liquid, brush over the demarcated area and sprinkle with the gravel.

To complete the cake, paint clouds in the sky with vegetable colouring and shade the water surface so that it does not appear too flat and blue.

The side of the cake may be left undecorated or have only a few decorations, as simplicity is the decisive factor – too much ornamentation will draw attention away from the main design on top of the cake and be excessive.

Modelling and dressing figures

Mould the head, pressing the paste firmly into the mould. Insert a toothpick through the neck into the head, leaving about 20 mm ($\frac{3}{4}$ in.) protruding. Set aside to dry.

Mould a piece of flower paste into the shape of a pear (*fig. 6A*). Cut a slit into the pointed end, measuring one and a half times the length of the head (*fig. 6B*). Shape the legs, with the knees about one head's length from the bottom. Shape the feet.

Push a piece of wire horizontally through the

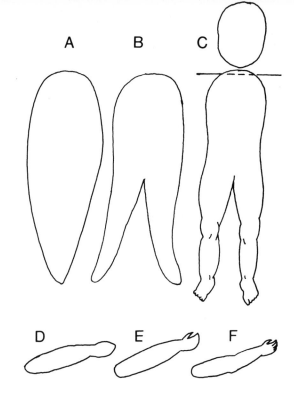

top of the body, leaving about 3 mm ($\frac{1}{8}$ in.) protruding on either side (*fig. 6C*)

Shape the body into the desired posture by bending the knees, torso, etc. If you wish it to stand upright, insert short lengths of florist's wire into the legs, leaving about 10 mm ($\frac{3}{8}$ in.) to 20 mm ($\frac{3}{4}$ in.) protruding at the feet.

Affix the head to the body and set aside to dry.

To make the arms, roll a small piece of paste into a sausage and flatten one end into a paddle shape (*fig. 6D*). The paddle (= the hand) should be the same length as the face from the chin to the middle of the forehead.

Cut a wedge from the paddle to form the thumb (*fig. 6E*), then cut out the other four fingers and roll them all into shape (*fig. 6F*). With the back of a scalpel or knife, make an incision in the hand just below the fingers and fold them inwards to look natural and relaxed. Alternatively, if required, shape the hand and fingers as if holding something, a bunch of flowers, for example.

Shape the forearm and upper arm, with the elbow about one head's length away from the hand (*fig. 6F*). (*Note:* The whole arm measures about one and a half times the length of the head. Be sure to make a pair of arms, one left and one right arm.)

Bend the arms as desired and make a hole in each at shoulder level with the wires protruding from the body. Allow to dry separately on a piece of sponge or wadding.

When everything is completely dry, the figure can be dressed. For a little girl, make the back of the dress first. Roll out a piece of flower paste very thinly and cut it out, using *fig. 7A* as a pattern. Brush a 2 mm ($\frac{1}{16}$ in.) wide strip of egg white along the seam edges, taking care not to get any egg white on the right side of the paste. Attach the paste to the back of the body, draping it as desired. Repeat procedure for the front, placing the seam edges over those of the back. Smooth the seams with the heel of a veining tool to make them as inconspicuous as possible.

Cut a sleeve out of a piece of rolled-out flower paste (*fig. 7B*) and brush a 2 mm ($\frac{1}{16}$ in.) wide strip of egg white along the inside edge of the back part of the seam. Attach the sleeve to an arm and fold it over, joining and smoothing the front and back seam parts as described in the previous step. Dress the other arm in the same way.

Brush a small ball of flower paste liberally with egg white and press it over the protruding wire at the right shoulder. Apply some egg white to the right arm around the hole and attach the arm to the body, forming a "mortise and tenon joint". Brush the inside edge of the sleeve head with egg white and join it very neatly to the armhole of the dress. Repeat the procedure for the left arm, and set aside to dry.

Cut out the collar (*fig. 7C*) and attach it with egg white.

To dress a little boy, cut out two of the trousers pattern (*fig. 8A*), one for the left and one for the right leg. First attach one of the legs, joining and smoothing the seam as described for the sleeves, then apply egg white to the centre front, centre back and waist of the body, and attach the top part of the pants. Repeat the procedure for the other leg.

Cut out two of the shirt pattern (*fig. 8B*). Attach first the back and then the front. Cut out and attach the collar (*fig. 8C*). Cut out and attach two sleeves (*fig. 7B*).

Note
These patterns are very simple and may either be elaborated upon or trimmed with pockets, cuffs, ties, etc.

Moulds

Either use commercial moulds, or make your own using plaster of Paris, quick-setting putty or ceramic clay. Taking a doll as an example, this is how you go about it:

Plaster of Paris mould
Grease the doll well with vegetable fat or petroleum jelly and place it in a hollow container, securing it in position with wonder putty.

Fill the container with pottery clay reaching halfway up the body of the doll.

Mix some plaster of Paris according to the manufacturer's instructions and pour it slowly over the doll, covering it completely. Tap the container lightly on the table to remove all air bubbles.

Set aside for at least 30 minutes to dry, then unmould.

To make a mould for the other half of the doll, repeat the procedure, but place the doll upside down.

Note
Remove the doll's arms and legs before making the moulds, as they are later shaped freehand to comply with requirements of the design.

This method is suitable only for figures with a uniform shape.

Ceramic clay or putty mould
Rub your hands with vegetable fat or petroleum jelly and knead the clay or putty well, until it is soft and pliable.

Grease the doll with vegetable fat or petroleum jelly.

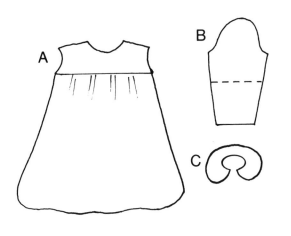

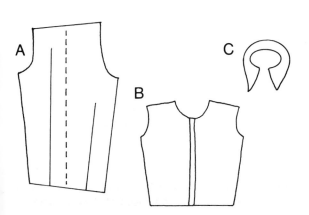

Fig. 7
Dress, collar and sleeve pattern for a girl

Fig. 8
Front/back, collar and pants pattern for a boy

25

Press the putty over the one half of the doll, making sure that all hollows are filled, otherwise certain features will be indistinct.

Leave on the doll until almost set, then remove very carefully, taking care that the mould does not lose its shape. Set aside to harden completely.

Repeat for the other half of the doll.

Crimping

This technique, although relatively slow, is very effective for decorating the tops and sides of cakes. Special instruments called crimpers, which resemble large tweezers, are used (*see plate 7*).

Crimpers come in various shapes and sizes, and are used, for example, to make long, medium or short straight or curved lines, heart and diamond patterns, etc.

Get patterns and templates ready before covering the cake with fondant, so that you can prick out and crimp the design immediately. If crimping is applied to fondant which has already become too hard, it will result in cracking or leave unsightly marks. In addition, once a crimping imprint has been made, it cannot be removed. It would be best, therefore, to practise with whatever crimpers you intend using on a partly covered dummy cake before tackling the actual work.

Note: Do not practise on a flat surface, as the skill mastered in this way differs from that required for working at an angle.

Make sure that the crimper you are going to use is clean and completely dry. If it is not, the fondant will stick to it. To prevent this from happening while you are working, dip the crimper in cornflour or fat at regular intervals.

Ensure that the prongs are about 5 mm ($\frac{1}{4}$ in.) apart and hold the crimper at right angles to the cake. Push the crimper into the fondant (not more than 3 mm ($\frac{1}{8}$ in.) deep), and squeeze until the prongs are approximately 1,5 mm ($\frac{1}{20}$ in.) apart. Release the pressure and allow the prongs to return to the 5 mm ($\frac{1}{4}$ in.) position. Remove the crimper.

Note: Remove the crimper when the gap between the prongs is exactly 5 mm ($\frac{1}{4}$ in.) wide – no more, no less. If it is removed at the wrong time, the crimper could pull out bits of the fondant or form holes.

A good idea would be to wind a rubber band or sticky tape around the crimper, about 20 mm ($\frac{3}{4}$ in.) from the front. This would prevent it from opening up more than 5 mm ($\frac{1}{4}$ in.)

Crimping should always be overpiped, using either the main colour of the cake or one that complements it. Crimping combines well with inserted ribbons, dropped loops, and bridge work, embroidery or lacework. *Plate 8* gives designs to use when decorating sides and/or tops of cakes.

Filigree and lacework

Filigree and lacework are extremely intricate, delicate patterns piped with royal icing, using tubes Nos. 1, 0 or 00. An injection needle attached to a tube can also be used. The piping is done on wax paper or a sheet of thin plastic (*not* clingfilm) secured over a pattern, and left to dry. It is then carefully removed and attached to the cake as a free-standing design.

Although some decorators finish off certain designs with cotton net or tulle, the result is far more striking and rewarding if filigree or lace made of royal icing is used.

Recipe for royal icing for filigree and bridge work
1 egg white, at room temperature
± 200 g (7 oz) icing sugar (± 400 ml)

Plate 7
Crimpers (note how the prongs of those in front are kept the correct distance apart with adhesive tape)

Plate 8
Progressives of seven crimping designs (continued on *plate 9*)

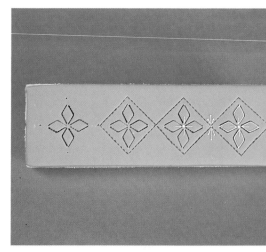

Plate 9
Continuation of *plate 8*

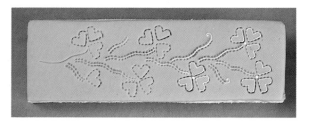
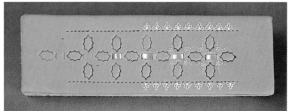
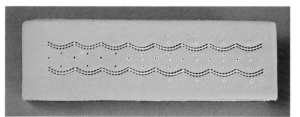
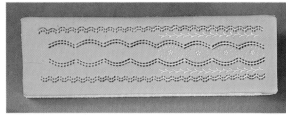
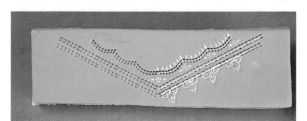
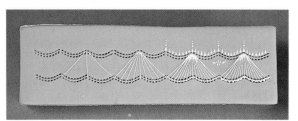
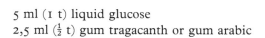

5 ml (1 t) liquid glucose
2,5 ml ($\frac{1}{2}$ t) gum tragacanth or gum arabic

Strain the egg white through a dry muslin cloth to break it up without affecting its ability to thicken. Beat lightly.

Sift the icing sugar through a very fine sieve (a piece of organdie or nylon stocking could also be used). Add gradually to the egg white, stirring continuously. Add just enough icing sugar to obtain a mixture with a soft, creamy consistency. Mix in the glucose and gum.

Test: The mixture is the right consistency if a spoon dipped into it and then lifted out leaves a smooth stiff peak that holds its shape in the icing. (If the mixture is too soft, the peak will curl back; if too much icing sugar has been added, the peak will break off.)

If the icing is too stiff, dip a spatula into it and coat it thinly, then dip the spatula into strained, beaten egg white. Mix this into the icing, repeating the procedure until the correct consistency is reached.

Royal icing should be snow-white in colour. (If it is not mixed correctly, it will look slightly creamy.) To make royal icing even brighter, dip the tip of the brush handle into blue colouring and mix the colouring into the icing.

Royal icing for filigree work should not be stored for any length of time, but used on the day it is made. Mix small batches for immediate use, halving the quantities of ingredients given in the recipe. Be extra careful to get the consistency right: if the mixture is too stiff, the fine piped lines will not stick to each other and if it is too soft, the lines will spread.

Do not
☐ sift the icing sugar too long before mixing it with the egg white, as lumps may form;
☐ use an electric beater to make the icing, as too much air will be incorporated – burst air bubbles mar the appearance of the piping.

Hint: Here's a way to ensure that the icing sugar is fine and lump-free. Stretch a piece of silk or nylon cloth over a small glass or plastic jar and spoon 15 ml (3 t) of icing sugar onto it. Seal with a tight-fitting lid and shake the container vigorously.

Remove the lid carefully, keeping the cloth taut to prevent it from slipping into the jar. Pour the sifted icing sugar into a clean, dry container and shake off the grains clinging to the cloth into another bowl. Take care not to mix up the two.

Repeat until you have enough sifted icing sugar. (Keep leftover grains for making butter icing.)

Guidelines
The secret to successful filigree and lacework lies in practise and careful but confident handling of completed pieces. Make two or three times as many pieces as you need for the cake; if you know you have enough spares, you will feel less

Plate 10
Handling filigree work
with a paintbrush

anxious about assembling them and will probably not break any!

The first step is to draw the pattern on a piece of paper (see *fig. 87 to 92,* page 132 for examples). When making original designs, remember to incorporate enough supporting lines, i.e. avoid long unconnected lines and introduce scrolls and coils with as many points of contact as possible.

Grease a metal disc or a piece of glass lightly with vegetable fat or white margarine. Place the pattern on top, grease and cover it with a piece of wax paper (you may use plastic instead, but then do not grease the pattern). Grease the wax paper or plastic too with a very thin layer that cannot be scraped off or absorbed by the piped icing (this will result in breakage).

Secure the greased wax paper or plastic with sticky tape to prevent it from moving during piping.

Using a No. 00 tube and royal icing, first pipe the trellis lines, then the lines that will join them together, taking care to connect *all* the trellis and connecting lines. Using a No. 0 tube, complete the decorative parts of the design, ending with the short supporting curved or straight lines. Over-pipe where necessary.

Leave to dry completely.

The most difficult part of filigree work is removing the piped design from the wax paper or plastic. There are various methods, but all require practice and experience.

Using wax paper

Place the metal disc, piping and all, in a moderately warm oven to melt the fat. Test with a fine brush: as soon as you can move the piped work, remove the disc carefully from the oven and place it on a flat surface. Slide a thin, firm strip of paper very carefully underneath the filigree work, from one side to the other, until the whole piece is on the paper. Keep the paper flat as you move it along and *do not lift it.* Or:

Melt the fat in a moderately warm oven as described above. Place a thin strip of sponge over the piped filigree work, slip one hand under the disc and, supporting the icing with your other hand, carefully turn it over so that the piping lies face down on the sponge. Remove the metal disc, then strip off the wax paper *very* carefully. Or:

Remove the piping and disc from the oven once the fat has melted and place it on a table. Loosen the wax paper, grip one end firmly and slide it off the disc, with the piping. Move it to the table edge so that the piping protrudes slightly. Slip

the fingertips of one hand between the wax paper and filigree work and, supporting the icing with this hand, slowly pull the paper down with the other to separate the two and end up with the icing on the supporting hand. This method is for those who like to live dangerously – if you do, wear medical gloves to prevent dampness on your hands from damaging the icing.

Using plastic

This method does not require heating. Simply loosen the plastic with the piped design from the metal disc, place it face down on a piece of sponge and gently peel off the plastic, leaving the design on the sponge.

Before assembling the pieces on the cake, over-pipe the lines that join the various sections together. Remember to take hold of the pieces where they are at their most solid to avoid breaking the filigree. You could also use the handle of a thin paintbrush, as shown in *plate 10.*

Freehand filigree and lacework can also be done on net nails and metal plates (see *fig. 9*).

Built-up line work

Built-up line work is done directly onto the cake using Nos. 0 and 00 tubes and royal icing.

Prick out the design on the fondant (see *plate 11* for a pattern).

Starting in the middle of a section, work from top to bottom: pipe three vertical lines about 2 mm ($\frac{1}{16}$ in.) apart, the middle one slightly longer than the other two. Repeat this piping in sections to match right around the cake.

Return to the first three lines and pipe another

Fig. 9
Net nails and metal
plates for filigree
lacework

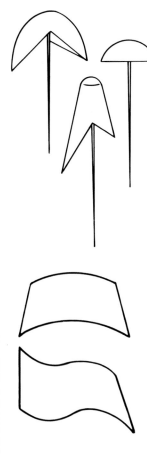

three lines (the same length) over them, but this time diagonally from right to left (see *plate 11*). Repeat for other piped lines.

The next step is to pipe three lines from left to right over the previous two sets of lines to obtain a grid with vertical and diagonal, but *no horizontal*, lines.

Return to the first section again. Pipe a fourth set of lines in exactly the same position as the first set, i.e. running from top to bottom, but lengthening each line on either end by about 2 mm ($\frac{1}{16}$ in.). Add an extra line on either side, piping five lines in all. Repeat all around the cake. Do the same in both diagonal directions, ending up with six layers of lines.

Note: Ensure that each line is exactly in line with the one beneath it, otherwise you will lose the grid effect.

Continue lengthening and adding on lines until the pattern spaces have been completely filled (see *plate 11*).

When piping *ovals*, lengthen the two sets of diagonal lines by 3 to 4 mm ($\frac{1}{8}$ in.), and the vertical lines by 2 mm ($\frac{1}{16}$ in.). If you do not do this, you will end up with a round instead of an oval dome.

Note: Pipe the first five sets of lines with tube No. 0 and the rest with tube No. 00.

Hollow line work

This is done on wax paper, left to dry and then attached to the cake with royal icing.

Copy the design onto a sheet of paper (see *plate 12* for a pattern) and secure wax paper over it.

Using a No. 0 tube and royal icing and starting at the wide end of the shape, pipe the first line following the outline of the pattern. Pipe a similar line on the opposite side, joining them neatly at the point. Allow to dry.

Pipe a second line slightly off-centre over each of the first, working towards the middle of the design. Allow to dry.

Continue in this manner, shortening the lines time and again at the pointed end, until the built-up lines meet in the centre, forming an open-ended hollow shape (see *plate 12*).

When dry, pipe a row of dots over the join in the centre and the edge of the open end to finish off the design.

Note: If you do not let the lines dry before adding the next set, the whole structure will collapse.

Extension and bridge work

This technique, also known as "dropped string work" or "curtain borders", is a firm favourite, especially among Australian cake decorators.

Make sure that the extension work (see pattern in *plate 13*) never touches the cake board. It should be at least 4 mm ($\frac{1}{8}$ in.) above the board to prevent breakage should the board move.

To start, measure the circumference and height of the cake and cut a strip of wax paper accordingly, adding an extra 20 mm ($\frac{3}{4}$ in.) on one of the short sides to allow for overlapping.

Fold the paper in half (two short sides meeting) and fold 10 mm ($\frac{3}{8}$ in.) back on either side. Fold the whole in half again to obtain quarters. Successive folding will give you eighths, sixteenths and so on. The design will dictate how many folds you will need.

Draw a row of scallops 4 mm ($\frac{1}{8}$ in.) above the bottom edge of the folded wax paper, then draw a similar row of scallops above them. You could add a straight line instead of this second row of scallops. The distance from the top row of scallops will depend on the depth of the cake – 50 mm (2 in.) is the average distance between the top scallops/straight line and those at the bottom.

Exert sufficient pressure when drawing to ensure that the design will be clearly visible along the entire length of paper when unfolded.

Fold the wax paper around the cake and secure it with adhesive tape where the two 10 mm ($\frac{3}{8}$ in.)

strips overlap. Secure further by pressing pins into the points where the top scallops meet or, in the case of a straight line, at regular short intervals.

Prick the top and bottom lines out onto the cake, making sure that all the details have come through, for once the pattern has been removed, it is impossible to reposition it exactly over the original placing. Pull out the pins and remove the paper carefully.

Pipe beading, a snail's trail or small shell designs around the cake, below the lower edge of the pricked-out design. Pretty shells can be made

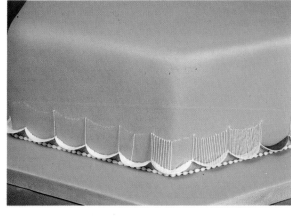

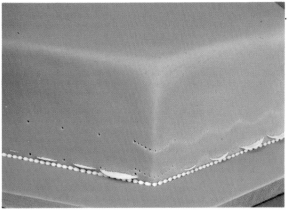

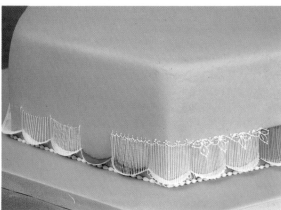

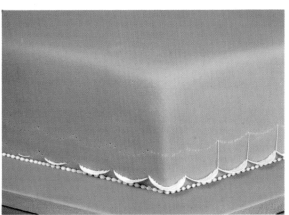

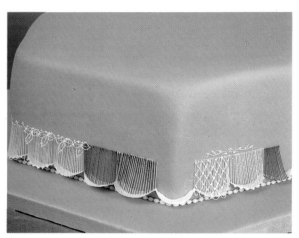

using Country Kitchen tubes, or Ateco tubes Nos. 13, 14 or 16, or a No. 42 Bekenal tube. This border will ensure that the extension work will be 4 mm ($\frac{1}{8}$ in.) or more above the board.

Using a No. 1, 0 or 00 tube and royal icing, begin piping the extension work in the *middle* of each bottom scallop: pipe a 10 mm ($\frac{3}{8}$ in.) line, moving around the cake until each scallop has this base line.

When dry, follow the outline of the pricked-out design and pipe a second line that touches both the cake and the first line and extends from 2 mm ($\frac{1}{16}$ in.) on the left to 2 mm ($\frac{1}{16}$ in.) on the right of the first line.

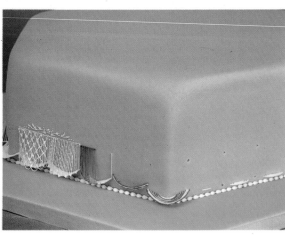

Continue piping in this manner until you reach the top of each scallop and they all meet at these corners (see *plate 13*).

Note: Each following line should be piped in such a way that the completed extension work, viewed from the front, presents the piped lines as a *straight* solid base. This can be achieved by placing them exactly in line as you work towards you. If placed off-centre, a cupped effect results. Also ensure that each line is at least partially dry before you apply the next one. If you work too quickly, the built-out scallop will either sag or collapse.

Six to nine piped lines in total are needed.

A bigger tube (No. 2 or 3) can be used to do extension work, but the result will not be as delicate.

Hint: Extension work can be finished off by flooding. Colour the royal icing to match the cake and the other decorations.

After completion, allow the extension work to dry completely, then do the bridge work:

Follow the recipe for royal icing given on page 16 (ingredients based on 1 egg white).

A No. 0 or 00 tube is generally used for bridge work, although experienced decorators could reach for an injection needle secured in the nose of an icing tube. Bridge work requires precision and a steady hand. It is hard on the eyes, so do not work at it for longer than 30 to 60 minutes at a time. Take a break every so often to lessen the strain on your eyes and rest your hand.

The top straight or scalloped line of the pattern serves as your guide. To start, pipe two vertical lines from the top of the design to the points on either side of a built-out scallop below.

Pipe a third line, reaching to the tip of the scallop, in the middle of the space formed by the first two lines. This is how you do it: place the tube on the top line of the design and, squeezing the icing bag, gradually move the nozzle down towards the extension work. For a neat finish, bring the tube over and around the edge to end underneath the built-out scallop.

Fill in the left-hand space with piped lines, leaving sufficient space between them for another line. Do the same in the right-hand space (see *plate 13*).

Repeat this procedure all around the cake and, when dry, fill the spaces with "dropped strings".

This method not only ensures that you can space lines evenly, but also enables you to remove broken or faulty lines relatively easily, using a paintbrush.

Finish off the top straight or scalloped line of the design with scrolls, beading or previously made lace points. Complete the bridge work with dots, over-piping or dropped lacework (see *plate 13*).

Double the bridge work by extending the built-up scallops (in the same way as they were originally formed) and piping strings from the top of the design, over the first set of strings, to the edge of the newly formed extension (see *plate 13*). Using a darker contrasting colour for the innermost set of bridges is particularly effective.

Collars

At the back of the book you will find three patterns for collars (see *fig. 83 to 86*). A rule of thumb to be considered at this stage is that, in the case of collars overlapping the edge of the cakes, best results will be obtained with cakes with a diameter of between 200 mm (8 in.) and 250 mm (10 in.). The diameter can, of course, be larger should you want the outer edge of the collar to rest on the edge of the cake.

However, for collar work the flood icing should not be too thick. I prefer a consistency based on the measure of seven counts (refer to the recipe on page 17). Do not overfill the pattern with flood icing – this will result in the design looking heavy and clumsy.

If the collar is bordered on the inner or outer edge with a strip or band, you must flood it first and only do the detail work or filigree once it has dried, to achieve an even whole. Before flooding the border band the outlines should be piped with royal icing and a No. 1 writing tube.

Then flood as follows: Start at a certain point, flooding 50 mm (2 in.) to the left and then 50 mm (2 in.) to the right; then continue with 50 mm (2 in.) to the left and 50 mm (2 in.) to the right. Repeat until completed. Should you follow a different procedure by working in one direction only, the join will be visible as the icing will have formed a crust by the time you finish.

Be very careful not to leave little air bubbles in the flood icing. Should any appear, break them immediately by pricking with a needle or the point of a brush, and smooth. If you don't do this, they may burst at a later stage and leave unsightly holes when the collar is completed and dry.

Hint: To ensure that the flood icing is level and even, tap the glass or board on which you are working on the table every now and then and place the finished article under a strong light or in front of a fan heater. This forms a crust quickly and makes the appearance smooth and shiny.

To obtain a neat and continuous line, place the pattern (secured on glass or a wooden board under thin plastic) on a turntable. Hold the icing bag in your right hand, with the elbow propped up on the table, and place the point of the writing tube on the pattern. Exert pressure on the icing bag while lifting the hand a few centimetres above the work surface. Hold the hand in this position while you maintain an even pressure on the bag and turn the turntable slowly with the left hand. This produces an even outline with only one join.

Miscellaneous decorations.

Lacework
Lace patterns are also to be found at the back of the book (see *fig. 150 to 152*). It is advisable to fill a whole sheet of these individual motifs at one time, as large quantities are usually attached to cakes. Trace the patterns very neatly onto grease-proof paper and secure on a board under thin plastic or under glass and proceed as follows:

Grease the plastic or glass with a very thin layer of vegetable fat.

Using a No. o writing tube and royal icing, pipe each motif neatly and accurately. Leave on the plastic or glass to dry thoroughly and store until required. Lift each piece very carefully off the plastic or glass and attach to the cake with royal icing.

Borders and embroidery
See *fig. 116 to 149* for patterns for this type of decoration. A No. o and/or 1 writing tube is usually used. If possible, pipe this freehand on the cake with the pattern as guide. A beginner will probably prefer the tracing method.

Determine the circumference of the cake and add 20 mm ($\frac{3}{4}$ in.) at both ends. Also measure the height of the cake and cut a corresponding strip of wax paper to fit neatly around the cake. Then decide how many times the pattern should be repeated (for example eight times). Fold the paper in half, again in half and then once more in half. Trace the pattern on the upper section of the folded paper, pressing hard to ensure that the design will show through all the layers. When you unfold the paper, the pattern will be distributed evenly. Wrap around the cake and pinprick the design onto the side of the cake on the fondant.

Pipe the design with royal icing over these marks, keeping the original pattern at hand to refer to where the pinpricks are a little indistinct. Be sure to cover all the pinprick marks.

Paste ribbon
The basis for this modelling paste (see recipe on page 18) can be mixed with a small amount of extra gum powder for greater elasticity and strength.

Roll the paste out until paper thin and transparent, then cut even strips, using a parsley cutter. For a finer or a narrower ribbon, these strips may be halved lengthways.

Fold loops to form the bow when you eventually assemble them. Pinch a reasonable portion of the end together and leave to dry as depicted on *plate 5*. Also shape the ends of the bows by curling and twisting them slightly. Use royal icing to assemble the bow. An example of the use of the ribbons can be seen on *plate 72*.

Should you want your ribbon to be glossy, brush with a glaze made of gum acacia powder (see recipe below). One layer will give you a very slight sheen, two or more will give you a high gloss. Each layer should be left to dry before applying the next or brushing with lustre dust.

Glaze
60 g (2 oz) gum acacia or gum arabic powder
125 ml ($\frac{1}{2}$ cup) cold water

Dissolve the gum in the water over a low temperature until completely melted and clear. Strain through a muslin cloth and store in the fridge in a screw-top jar. A few drops of brandy may be added to prevent the glaze from going off.

Sugar rocks
1 kg (2 lb 2 oz) granulated sugar
250 ml (1 cup) cold water
$\frac{1}{2}$ × recipe royal icing (see page 16)

Melt the sugar in the water over a low temperature and boil to 138 °C (280 °F). Remove from the stove and immediately stir in the very well-beaten royal icing. Pour into a shoe box or similar container, lined with well-greased wax paper. The mixture will bubble up to double its original volume. Leave to cool and then break up into required sizes (rocks).

To obtain coloured rocks, colour the royal icing beforehand.

For sand and gravel, crush the rocks with a rolling pin.

Glitter
Prepare the glaze mixture as described under paste ribbon above. Brush this mixture onto a clean porcelain or enamel surface. Dry in an oven at a low temperature. As soon as it is dry, remove from the oven and flake off. Store in an airtight jar.

For coloured glitter, mix colouring into the liquid glaze mixture before drying.

If you would like glitter on a Christmas tree or another object, the flakes can be crushed and the object dusted with it.

Rice-paper painting

Patterns for flood work (see *fig. 79 to 82,* as well as more detailed pictures are suitable for rice-paper painting. The technique is as follows:

Place the rice paper with the smooth side upwards over the pattern to be used. Trace every detail with a very fine felt-tipped pen. Brush this side with clear piping gel, using a No. 10 flat-tipped brush, applying even strokes in one direction. Do not criss-cross the gel over the design. The layer of gel should be very thin and extend about 50 mm (2 in.) beyond the outer edges of the pattern. (Incidentally, the gel is easily obtainable on the market.) Paint the picture with vegetable colouring while the gel is still wet, and allow to dry. Ensure that there are shades and highlights to obtain depth and dimension.

Leave to dry thoroughly.

Cut out carefully, leaving a frame of about 2 mm ($\frac{1}{16}$ in.) all round the picture. Turn over and cover the rough side of the rice paper with piping gel (once again with even strokes of the brush). Position the gelled side on the cake and press carefully with the handle of the brush to secure (only along the edge – do not press the centre as this could result in the rice paper tearing and spoiling the picture).

Cocoa painting

This technique is very similar to watercolour painting and is done with a mixture of cocoa powder and cocoa butter, or coconut oil, or white vegetable fat – never use any other colourings, as you then deviate from what the name implies. Cocoa painting can be done on rolled-out marzipan or plastic icing but not on pastillage, which is too porous. It is usually finished off with a frame or a border (*plates 89 and 99*).

Transferring a design onto a cake or plaque: Trace off the pattern (see *fig. 112* for an example), turn the paper over and copy the outlines in pencil. Place the traced-off pattern, right side up, on the surface of the cake or plaque (it should be completely dry) and go over the outlines again to get a transfer.

Mixing the cocoa paint: Melt a little cocoa butter or fat in three separate containers and add enough cocoa powder to each to obtain three tints: dark brown, medium brown and light brown. Keep them liquid on a hot tray or hotplate set to a very low temperature or over hot water.

Painting technique: Work from top to bottom. Copy the outlines of the first section with a fine brush and the darkest tint, then shade it in with all three tints to give depth to the drawing. Leave unpainted areas where you wish to add highlights. Repeat the procedure until the picture is complete, then study it critically and add a few finishing touches, or scrape off colouring to add more highlights where necessary. (*Hint:* If your design is a copy of a colour picture, keep the original handy to serve as guide for highlighting and shading.)

Flowers, ferns and fillers

Royal-icing flowers

Forget-me-nots

Cover a work board or cake drum with wax paper. Colour the icing bright blue, put in a piping bag with a No. 1 writing tube and pipe five dots (representing the flower petals) close together on the paper to form a circle.

First pipe a small dot at the top to represent the first petal, then pipe two dots slightly lower down on either side of it. Pipe another two dots directly under these to complete the circle. Finally, pipe a small yellow dot with a No. 1 writing tube in the centre (see *plate 14*).

When completely dry these can be attached to a small piece of wire for use in flower arrangements. They can also be used on the sides of cakes as part of embroidery work or piped directly onto the cake.

Rosebuds

These pretty little rosebuds (about 10 mm [$\frac{3}{8}$ in.] in diameter) are very useful for embroidery patterns on a cake.

Put a small amount of royal icing on a rose nail and attach a square piece of wax paper (see *plate 14*). Use a No. 73 or 74 Errington tube and the desired colour of royal icing. Place the wide end of the tube on the wax paper on the nail, with the indentation towards you. Don't hold the tube too firmly against the rose nail as it will be impossible to turn the nail.

Hold the tube in an upright position. Press the piping bag with the right hand while you turn the rose nail in the left hand in an anti-clockwise direction to form a spiral (the centre of the flower). This spiral must be pointed at the top.

Turn the rose nail so that the end of the spiral will be in the ten-o'clock position. Place the wide end of the tube in the twelve-o'clock position at the base of the spiral, with the narrow end slightly towards the outside and the tube at an angle of approximately 45°. Press the bag and turn the rose nail anti-clockwise, but form only a half circle. Lift off.

Place the tube against the base of the petal in the same way to overlap it by approximately one-third. Turn the rose nail while you press the bag to form another half circle.

Leave to dry thoroughly. Hold the rose bud in your left hand, with the flat side towards you. Pipe five dots in green royal icing with a No. 2 tube around the base. Place the tube in the centre of these dots, and press the bag for a few seconds to form the hip. Continue squeezing while you move your hand away gradually to form the stem. Place on its side on a piece of wax paper to dry.

To make a larger rose of about 30 mm ($1\frac{1}{4}$ in.) in diameter (see *plate 14*), make a cone with a No. 7 or 8 star tube (on wax paper on a rose nail). Leave to dry. Pipe a little spiral around the upper tip of the cone with a No. 71 or 69 Errington tube, then pipe three semi-circular petals around it as described for the rosebud. Form five similar petals lower down, and leave to dry. This is now ready for use (it is not necessary to make a calyx and stem).

These roses can be made in butter icing as well.

Blossoms

Very small blossoms made with a No. 73 or 74 Errington tube can be used effectively in embroidery. Use a No. 71 or 72 Errington tube or No. 42 Tala tube, if you have one, to make larger blossoms. (Unfortunately, the Tala tube is no longer available on the market.)

Place a small piece of wax paper with royal icing on a rose nail. Position the wide end of the petal tube on the nail, with the indentation towards you. Hold the tube at an angle of 45° to ensure that the petals will not be too thick or curl too much.

Turn the nail in an anti-clockwise direction in your left hand while you squeeze the bag. Do not move your right hand. As soon as the petal has been formed, stop squeezing and lift off the tube.

Put the wide end of the tube slightly underneath the first petal and repeat the last procedure. Form three more petals in the same way so that there will be five petals overlapping each other in a circle (see *plate 14*).

Allow to dry. Push one end of a No. 26 florist's wire through the middle of the flower. Pipe a small amount of green royal icing into the centre and press in yellow nonpareils to form stamens, or use artificial stamens that vary in length. The base of the petals can be painted with a darker colour for effect before the stamens are inserted. Paint the tips of the stamens with colouring.

Green royal icing can be substituted for florist's wire to form the stem (see instructions under rosebuds).

Small daisy (about 20 mm [¾ in.] in diameter)
Use a No. 1 writing tube to form the petals, again using the rose nail and a piece of wax paper.

Form a series of "teardrops" with the wide end towards the outside and the pointed tips towards the inside (the tips must touch). Firstly pipe two tears opposite each other and then two in between to form a cross. Fill the spaces between the legs of the cross with matching drops to form a circle of eight petals.

Allow to dry slightly, then press the petals with the tip of the finger to flatten them (see *plate 14*). Prick a hole in the centre of the flower big enough for the insertion of a No. 26 florist's wire. Allow to dry completely. Bend the top end of the wire into a hook, then bend the hook over into a horizontal position.

Pipe a small amount of green royal icing into the centre of the flower, insert the wire and pull the hook into the icing. Dip into yellow nonpareils and leave to dry thoroughly.

Paint the centre of the flower with a little colouring around the stamens and also highlight some of the tips of the stamens.

Larger daisies (about 35 mm [1⅜ in.] in diameter)
These flowers (see *plate 14*) are made of individually piped petals which are assembled afterwards with royal icing.

Draw two parallel lines, about 20 mm (¾ in.) apart, on a piece of greaseproof paper. Draw a few more pairs of lines directly underneath, with spaces in between. Secure the pattern on a wooden board and cover with wax paper or thin plastic, as described earlier on.

Pipe tear drops between the lines with a No. 2 writing tube as for the small daisy. Flatten with the fingertip and draw a line with a pin for the vein. Leave to dry.

Pipe a small quantity of royal icing in the same colour as the petals onto a square of wax paper. Insert the petals to form a circle. Support these with two semi-circles of sponge or foam rubber (the thicker the sponge and the smaller the hole in the centre, the more closed the flower will be).

Make a hole in the centre while the icing is still soft to allow a wire stem to be inserted later on. Leave to dry.

Form a hook at the top end of a No. 24 florist's wire and bend over so that it will rest flat on the flower. Lift the flower carefully and push the wire stem through the hole. Cover the loop with yellow royal icing, taking care that a small amount of icing is underneath the hook. Pour nonpareils over the centre and shake off the excess. Leave to dry.

Paste flowers

Specific measurements and colours are mentioned in the following instructions. The intention is not to prescribe, but to give an indication of the proportions between the different components, as the size and colour of the flowers are to correspond with the colour scheme and arrangements on the cake.

Anonymous flower
Roll a small piece of modelling paste into a teardrop. Press the bottom half flat to form a Mexican hat shape. Place a five-petal blossom cutter of about 15 mm (⅝ in.) in diameter over the "hat" and cut out. Lay on the palm of the hand with the point upwards and roll each petal with a ball modelling tool until very thin and slightly hollow.

Take the point of the flower in the left hand and press a little star into the trumpet with a fluted modelling tool (see *plate 15*). Draw the veins on the petals from the centre to the tip of each petal with a dressmaker's pin or a veiner and make a hole through the trumpet. Tape three stamens of varying lengths to the top end of a piece of No. 26 florist's wire and push this through the trumpet.

Press the paste securely onto the stem and pinch each petal slightly to curl them backwards. Paint the tips of the stamens pink.

These flowers can be used individually, or taped together in a spray.

Blossoms

Colour the modelling paste as desired and roll very thinly. Cut out a shape using the same cutter as for the anonymous flower. Roll each petal very thinly with a ball tool and mark the divisions between each petal with a hat pin or dressmaker's pin. Press a small hole in the centre and insert a stamen which will serve as the stem. Secure with royal icing or egg white.

Paint the centre of the flower with colouring and leave to dry thoroughly. Now make a few buds as follows (see *plate 15*).

Roll a small amount of modelling paste into a ball. Flatten and press the head of a stamen onto this with egg white. Roll between the fingers to form a small teardrop, about the same length as the radius of the flower. Leave to dry.

Tape the buds and flowers into sprays of your choice onto No. 26 florist's wire as described on pages 42 to 43 under *Cymbidium*.

Apple blossom

Form a small piece of green modelling paste into a Mexican hat shape. Cut out the calyx with a tiny star cutter, about 10 mm ($\frac{3}{8}$ in.) in diameter. Hold the calyx by the stem in your left hand and roll out each petal thinly with a small glass-tipped pin. Hollow the calyx slightly. Prick a hole through the centre of the calyx and through the stem with the pin, and insert a stamen without a head, leaving a small section sticking out at the front. Secure with egg white.

Roll out a small piece of white paste until almost transparent and cut out five petals, about 10 mm ($\frac{3}{8}$ in.) in diameter, with a small petal cutter.

Place a petal on the palm of the hand and roll each petal with a small ball tool until very thin and transparent. Vein from the outer top edge of the petal to the point with a pin or veiner.

When all five petals have been formed in the same way arrange them on the calyx and secure with egg white. These petals should be arranged between the leaves of the calyx so that a small green star is formed in the centre. Leave to dry and dust the back of the petals with pink chalk.

Pipe a small quantity of green royal icing into

the centre and insert about 14 stamens without tips into this. Paint the tips of the stamens with pink colouring.

Mock orange

This little flower is made in exactly the same way as the apple blossom in *plate 15*, with the following exceptions:
☐ the calyx cutter has only four points;
☐ there are only four white petals which are fixed onto each leaf of the calyx and not between;
☐ the stamens are decreased by about a half; and
☐ the flowers are left white, except for the tips of the stamens which may be painted pink.

Jasmine

Start the flowers with a Mexican hat shape in white modelling paste (see *plate 15*). Use the same cutter as for the anonymous flower but roll the petals into a long and pointed shape. The stem of the flower must be longer than the anonymous flower – about one-third longer than the diameter of the flower. Hollow each petal on the back with a ball tool.

Prick through the centre and the stem with a pin, and insert a stamen with a small head, leaving about 4 mm ($\frac{1}{8}$ in.) of the stamen protruding at the top. Enlarge the hole in the centre of the flower with a No. 32 Anger modelling tool. Roll the stem between the two index fingers, moving downwards to secure the paste to the stem and tapering it slightly towards the bottom. The paste will move upwards on the stamen, eventually leaving only the protruding tip of the stamen. Leave to dry, then dust the stem and the trumpet with pink chalk. Do not dust the back of the petals.

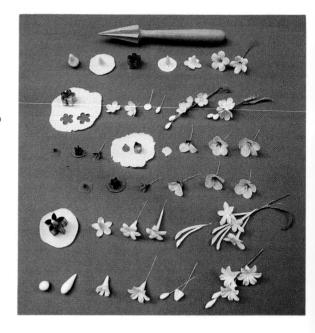

Plate 15
How to make the anonymous flower, blossoms, apple blossom, mock orange, jasmine and hyacinth of modelling paste (a fluted modelling tool is depicted on the top)

Make more flowers and make the buds as follows: roll a tiny piece of modelling paste around a stamen dipped in egg white, a little longer than the completed flowers. Taper towards the stem end, and thicken slightly at the top, ending with a point. Leave to dry and dust with the same pink chalk.

Tape together as for the blossom (in the last paragraph).

Hyacinth

Shape the required colour of modelling paste into a teardrop, with the thicker end about 7 mm ($\frac{1}{4}$ in.) in diameter. Press the wide end of the teardrop with the back of a small paintbrush and hollow it to form a small trumpet (see *plate 15*).

Make six cuts around the trumpet and cut the tip of each petal to form a point. Lay on the palm of the hand with the stem upwards, and lengthen and thin each petal with a small ball tool. Pinch and pull backwards.

Turn over and press the fluted modelling tool into the centre. Mark the veins on each petal with a pin or special veiner. Insert a stamen to form the stem and press the paste firmly onto this to taper it. Leave to dry.

Make buds with a tiny piece of modelling paste. Flatten into a small triangle and place the tip of a stamen dipped in egg white onto this. Roll into a teardrop shape that encloses the tip of the stamen. This must be about the same length as that of an individual flower petal. Dry thoroughly and tape together as for the blossoms.

Daisy

Roll the modelling paste out thinly, and cut the shape out with an eight-petalled cutter, about 35 mm ($1\frac{3}{8}$ in.) in diameter. Cut each petal in half lengthways leaving the centre intact.

Spread the sixteen petals evenly in a circle and press these flat with a No. 32 Anger tool to form the flower petals (see *plate 16*).

Make a small hole in the centre of the flower that will be large enough for the florist's wire later on. Place the flower on acrylic cottonwool, press with the ball end of a modelling tool to shape and leave to dry thoroughly.

Pipe a small amount of yellow royal icing over the hole. Insert a covered No. 26 wire with a small hook at the top end and pull onto this icing.

Dust the base of the petals with green chalk. Pipe a small amount of royal icing over the hook in the centre and dip the flower into yellow non-pareils. Leave to dry.

Make a very small Mexican hat shape from green modelling paste and cut out a calyx about 15 mm ($\frac{5}{8}$ in.) in diameter. Wet the back of the flower with egg white, push the stem through the calyx and secure against the flower.

Sweetpea

Special cutters to make sweetpeas are obtainable from cake-decorating shops (see *plate 16*).

The first step in assembling this flower is to cover a short length of No. 26 florist's wire with tape (see description on pages 42 to 43 under *Cymbidium*). Tape a short stamen to the top end of the wire.

Roll out a small piece of prepared coloured paste very thinly and mould around the wire in a slightly rounded crescent shape.

Press out a shape in the same colour paste with a petal cutter and cut in half through the centre.

Attach these two halves on either side of the crescent shape with egg white and smooth the seam at the rounded end. The straight end will be open, revealing the centre.

Cut a butterfly shape out of the paste with the second cutter and lay on the palm of the hand. Thin the edges with the ball tool and ruffle. Turn over and pinch the centre on the back to form an indentation in the front. Brush this with egg white and press the modelled crescent shape flat against it. Fold slightly together to achieve a natural appearance and press to secure.

The next, slightly larger petal is cut out of thinly rolled paste with the third cutter. Ruffle and pinch on the back as for the previous petal. Wet the base of this petal with egg white and press the butterfly to the centre. Make sure that they are firmly secured and press the top of the petal over slightly to make it look soft and life-like.

Plate 16
How to make the daisy (top two lines) and sweetpea (bottom three lines) of modelling paste

To make the calyx, cut a small shape out of very thinly rolled out green modelling paste with a small star-shaped cutter, about 20 mm ($\frac{3}{4}$ in.) in diameter. Press the wire through the centre and secure with egg white to the bottom of the flower to form the calyx. Curl the tips back for a soft, natural appearance.

Make two more similar flowers.

Make a fourth flower by following all the steps mentioned above, but do not ruffle the edges of the "butterfly". (They should remain slightly flattened and secured more closely over the centre part of the flower to represent a flower which is half opened.)

Make a fifth flower, using all the illustrated stages. The layers are placed on top of each other to represent a flower that is just about to start opening. The sixth flower (a bud) is left completely closed and consists only of the rounded crescent and a petal shape that is cut with the first cutter.

Tape the bud to the top end of a No. 26 wire (covered), then tape the bud starting to open on the left. Then tape the half open flower slightly lower down on the right side of the stem. Now form a triangle with the three open flowers (two to the left and one to the right), leaving space between each flower down the stem. Finish off by covering the stalk neatly with tape.

Carnation

Roll out modelling paste very thinly and cut a scalloped shape from this with a cookie cutter (see *plate 17*). Make three or four shallow cuts around the edge of the scallop and a longer one of about 5 mm ($\frac{1}{4}$ in.) in each corner.

Use a No. 32 Anger tool or something similar in shape, and roll each cut scallop with the rounded section of the cone-shaped modelling stick (roll it backwards and forwards on the same spot) to ruffle the petals. Each section must be shaped and fluted separately and must not stick to another section, so as to form individual petals.

When completely shaped and ruffled, turn upside down on the work surface. Paint egg white carefully on the unruffled centre, taking care not to wet the petals. Fold in half, pressing only on the centre of the fold. Take care not to stick the two sections together too firmly.

Push the two corners on the sides towards the middle with the end of a brush, dividing the circle into quarters. Pick the flower up in the left hand, holding only the point between the fingers. Brush some more egg white between the folds, and press together with the finger tips to form a neat, round flower head.

Tape two long white stamens to the top end of a short length of No. 22 or 24 florist's wire. Press through the centre of the petals and pull through so that only the two stamens show above the petals. Press the paste firmly to the stem. If the bottom part of the flower is too long, shorten, and shape neatly and evenly around the wire stem. Leave to set thoroughly.

Cut a second pattern out of paste and follow the above procedure until the last step in the first row on the picture. In other words, do not fold together. Brush the smooth centre with egg white and insert the stem of the formed flower through the centre of the second pattern. Pleat the second row of petals around and underneath the first ones and press firmly to secure.

Trim off excess paste.

Roll out green modelling paste very thinly and cut into a rectangle with slightly slanted sides (refer to picture). Cut triangles across the upper edge of the rectangle to form the five leaves of the calyx. Roll each leaf on the underside with a ball tool to hollow slightly. Brush the uncut part with egg white and fold around the lower half of the flower. Press firmly, and smooth the join so that it is invisible.

Cut two very tiny petal shapes out of the same green modelling paste and hollow slightly with the ball tool. Attach at the bottom of the calyx on opposite sides of the flower. Shape two more similar petals that are slightly wider and a little shorter than the first two. Attach between the other two petals on opposite sides with egg white.

Roll a tiny piece of green paste between the fingers to form a sausage that is pointed at both ends and slightly thicker in the centre. Flatten slightly, stick the stem through the centre and attach to the calyx with egg white.

If the flower is to be used on a cake on its own, you can attach extra pairs of these leaves at intervals to the stem of the carnation.

Frangipani

Roll out white modelling paste to a thickness of about 1 mm ($\frac{1}{25}$ in.) and cut five petals with the frangipani cutter (see *plate 17*). Make sure that the rounded edge will be on your left side.

Place a petal on the palm of your hand and draw a line about 1 mm ($\frac{1}{25}$ in.) from the edge of the rounded side on the inside. Roll the edge towards you and ball with a modelling tool just inside this "roll" to cup slightly. Position diagonally over the handle of a wooden spoon, from left to right. Shape four more similar petals. Leave to set slightly (the paste must still be pliable for the next step).

Paint the lower points of the petals with yellow

vegetable colouring and assemble to form a fan of overlapping petals. Press together firmly and fold the left petal over to the right, with its cupped edge just inside that of the petal on the far right. Roll the uncupped edge of the right petal over to the left, bringing it around the back of the left petal. Twist the base of the flower slightly and unfold the petals so that they curve out like a natural flower.

Wet the one end of a No. 24 florist's wire with egg white and press into the base of the flower. Secure firmly.

Put the frangipani into a cone made from a square piece of aluminium foil (cut the square through from one corner to the centre, then fold the one point over the other to form a cone). Cut a hole in the bottom of the foil and curl the edges slightly to the outside. Push the stem of the flower through the hole and place over a little spice bottle, with the stem hanging inside it. The petals should rest on the upper rounded edge of the cone.

Leave to dry and dust the inside of the petals with yellow chalk. Turn upside down and draw veins lengthways over the petals with pinkish-brown chalk. Colour the base of the flower with brown and green chalk.

If you would like buds for your arrangement, proceed as follows:

Form an elongated teardrop over a length of covered florist's wire. Make five cuts from one point of the drop to the other around this. Holding each end between the thumb and index finger of both hands, twist the teardrop, turning the hands in opposite directions. Leave to dry.

Open rose

The rose depicted in the top two rows of *plate 18* consists of five petals and the calyx.

Roll out pale pink modelling paste until almost transparent. Cut out five petals with a little cutter. Cover the balance of the rolled-out paste with a piece of plastic to prevent it from drying out.

Ruffle the outer edges of the petals with a ball modelling tool on the palm of your hand. Take care that the outer edges of the petals in particular are very thin.

Grease a table tennis ball with white vegetable fat. Press the petals against this so that the lower halves stick to the ball. The upper edges can now be curled or fluted as desired. Leave to dry.

Cut a very small calyx in the same colour paste that was used for the flowers, with the radius about one-third of the length of the petals. Put in an individual polystyrene apple container and attach the dry petals to it with egg white. First overlap two petals, then attach one on the opposite side. The two remaining petals are now secured in the two spaces between the petals that have already been attached.

They should all overlap.

Pipe a small quantity of yellow royal icing in the centre where the petals meet. Insert a length of No. 22 or 24 covered florist's wire with a flattened hook at the top and pull into the royal icing.

Leave to dry.

Pipe a small quantity of yellow royal icing in a circle around the wire hook and press 45 to 50 or more artificial stamens into it. Finish off the flower neatly with a small dot of icing in the centre of the circle. Paint the tips of the stamens with brown, orange or dark-pink colouring.

If you dust the centre of the flower with a darker shade of chalk before inserting the stamens, you add depth to your flower.

Roll out separate pieces of white and green paste very thinly. Press the white onto the green and roll out firmly. Cut a calyx from this with a radius approximately two-thirds that of the petals. Mould the tips with a ball tool (see picture).

Push the stem of the flower through the centre of the calyx and attach to the base of the flower with egg white.

Roll a small ball of green paste around the stem below the calyx to form the hip.

Cécile Brunner rose

This rose is made from three tints of the same colour (see the last three rows of *plate 18*, and refer to page 19 on how to colour modelling paste).

Plate 17
How to make the carnation (top three lines) and the frangipani (bottom three lines) of modelling paste

39

Plate 18

How to make the open
rose (top two lines)
and the Cécile Brunner
rose (bottom three
lines) of modelling
paste

These roses are particularly effective on christening cakes and in dainty floral arrangements. Keep them small to enable them to look as close to nature as possible. Although one can use up to twenty petals to form this rose, the diameter should not be more than 30 mm (1¼ in.).

Use a small ball of paste in the darkest tint and shape in a sausage about 30 mm (1¼ in.) long and 5 mm (¼ in.) in diameter.

Roll the sausage flat on the one side with a modelling tool until very fine and transparent. The base should remain fairly thick as this is going to form the bud of the rose. Do not allow it to become crescent shaped (refer to picture).

Bend a hook on one end of a piece of No. 24 florist's wire. Brush the lower, thick base of the rolled-out paste with egg white, put the hook on this and roll up as for a Swiss roll. The upper edge should be kept as straight as possible. Secure by pressing the thickened base firmly onto the wire. Fold the free end of the roll slightly so that it curls back.

Use the second colour to form the next three to five small petals in this way: Place a small ball of paste, about 4 mm (⅛ in.) in diameter, on your work surface and flatten on one side to form a rose petal shape. Mould with the ball tool until the petal is as long as the bud and very thin around the edge. This should never be longer or shorter than the bud. If you find it necessary, use a pair of scissors to trim to shape.

Lay this petal on the side of the palm of your hand, in line with the little finger, and hollow the centre with the ball tool, which will curl and ruffle the outer edge.

Brush only the lower edge of the petal with egg white and press the completed bud against the petal so that only the base is attached. It is essential that the whole upper portion of the petal is free from the bud to facilitate curling and bending. Do not turn these petals back too much at this stage as additional petals have to be attached to complete the rose.

Add another three to five petals in the same way in a circle around the bud to overlap each other by approximately one-third. The outer petals must be made in the palest tint.

The width of the petals may differ, but they should always be of the same height, otherwise the centre of the rose will be too high and the petals too low on the stem to look natural.

Never attach more than five of these petals in one stage to prevent the centre from being pressed out at the top. When you handle the flower, do not press in the centre of the petals when you attach them as this will form a little "waist" which will make the rose resemble a tulip. The flower should always be held just below the base by the stem while you work on it.

Attach the calyx when completely dry. The calyx cutter that is available for this purpose is a little clumsy for this flower. Roll out a piece of green paste very thinly until about 100 mm (4 in.) to 120 mm (4¾ in.) long and 15 mm (⅝ in.) wide. Cut into wedges as indicated in the picture and attach one by one to the base of the rose. (I usually do not curl these leaves back as their tips are inclined to break off easily. I stick them against the rose for safety's sake.)

Finally, form a very small ball of green paste about 2 mm (1/16 in.) in diameter and mould it around the stem below the leaves of the calyx to form the rose hip.

Tea rose

Three tints of the same colour are used for this rose as well, but unlike the Cécile Brunner rose the starting point is a cone.

Before forming the cone decide what the size of the completed rose should be. The cone is always about 20 mm (¾ in.) shorter than the actual rose. If a rose is 50 mm (2 in.) high, for example, the cone should not be longer than 30 mm (1¼ in.), and the thickest point should have a diameter of about 7 mm (¼ in.).

The first petals are slightly thicker and narrower than the final ones, but they must all be of the same height. A template of this petal can be cut out of wax paper and kept at hand to serve as a sample to check the height of all the following petals. Note that the petals can be gradually rolled wider.

For this rose I use three to five petals in the first colour, about five in the next, and as many as required in the final tint to complete the rose. There is no hard and fast rule, however, for the number differs according to size.

The tea rose is quite a heavy flower and this means using a much heavier gauge of florist's wire for the stem (No. 18 is a good thickness). One end of the wire is turned into a hook. Form the cone around this and leave to dry thoroughly (see steps 1 and 2 on *plate 19*). Then attach the petals.

The first petal is formed with a very narrow tip and is about 20 mm (¾ in.) longer than the cone. Brush the bottom edge with egg white and fold around the cone. Attach firmly at the base.

Shape the second petal and attach on the opposite side in the same way.

The third petal should be rolled slightly wider and much thinner than the first two. Lift one side of the second petal away from the bud and insert the petal between this and the bud, as deeply as possible. Brush egg white over the bottom edge.

Shape one or two more petals and attach them in the same way. The top edges of these petals may be curled back slightly, but do not curl the first two. Leave to dry at this stage.

The next series of petals are made in the second tint of your colour. You can also use a cutter for this purpose. (I find it more satisfactory to use a piece of modelling paste shaped into a cone and then flattened and moulded into a petal with a modelling tool.) The base of these petals should be slightly thicker, which ensures a good appearance.

If the dry petals make it difficult to attach the

next lot, cut a crescent shape out of the lower half of the petal and insert the point between the dry petals to make it look as though this petal unfolds between the previous ones. Secure with egg white and smooth the join. It is not necessary for the last few petals to overlap each other. Curl and bend their edges to look as natural as possible.

Leave to dry completely.

Make the calyx and the rose hip as follows: Roll out a piece of white and a piece of green modelling paste thinly, place together and roll out again. Cut out the calyx and roll each leaf separately until long and very thin. Use a scalpel and make one or two cuts on the side of each leaf.

With the white uppermost, roll each leaf with a ball tool to hollow slightly. Attach a small ball of green paste to the base of the rose. Stick the stem through the middle of the calyx and attach it to the base of the rose with egg white. Mould the calyx carefully around the piece of paste at the base of the rose to form the hip. Turn the calyx leaves over to reveal the white bloom.

Cover the wire with green paste to form the stem of the rose. Use light-brown paste and shape the thorns into a triangle, with the sharp tips slightly curved and the base fairly thick and wide. Attach to the stem with egg white.

Make the stem leaves by rolling out green modelling paste very thinly. Attach a very thin green-covered florist's wire to it with egg white, then put a second layer of rolled-out green paste over the wire on the first layer. Use a leaf cutter and cut out. Mould the edges with a modelling stick to curl slightly, then press on an artificial or fresh leaf to create veins. Make more leaves in the same way. There should be three large ones and two slightly smaller ones.

Leave to dry completely then assemble as follows:

Use a No. 24 wire covered with florist's tape and attach one of the larger leaves to the top. Attach the two remaining large leaves opposite each other slightly lower on the stem, then the two smaller leaves lower down on the stem. Finally attach this composite leaf to the stem of the rose. You can also make another, or more, to attach to the stem.

Roll a piece of brown and a piece of green modelling paste together, cut a shape from this and attach to the base of the leaf stalk. The shape should be wider at the bottom, indented in the middle, narrow at the top, which must be cut to make it V-shaped. Place on top of the leaf-stalk at its base, with the broader side against the flower-stalk and attach firmly with egg white.

Plate 19
The tea rose (the cutter, bottom left, is for the making of stem-leaves)

Paint the edges of the leaves with red vegetable colouring, and dust the surface of the leaves in places with red chalk to break the green. The petals of the rose may also be dusted in places and around the edges with a deeper tint or contrasting colour to brighten it.

The tea rose can be used on its own or together with a bud and a half open rose on cakes or in arrangements. Always use odd numbers for good composition.

If you prefer, you can add a few dainty flowers like jasmine, hyacinths or blossoms.

These roses may also be tied together with ribbon made from flower paste for a softening effect, but do remember to keep to the minimum as it is the rose you want to exhibit, not the ribbon.

Cymbidium

These orchids can be made quite easily with the aid of two cutters (refer to *fig. 10*).

First cover a piece of No. 22 florist's wire with green florist's tape in the following way: Attach the free end of the tape firmly to one end of the wire. Hold the tape firmly between the thumb and index finger of the left hand, with the wire lying horizontally over the fingers and the hand (almost like a pencil). The tape will hang vertically between the fingers in the hollow of the hand. Hold the wire where the tape is attached between the thumb and index finger of the right hand and roll between these fingers. The tape should be held taut at an angle in the other hand

at the same time. It will then automatically be rolled around the length of the wire in a spiral.

Bend one end of the wire into a hook and curve about 20 mm ($\frac{3}{4}$ in.) of this end as indicated in the top line of *plate 20*. Mould a ball of white paste around this curve in the form of a teardrop. Pinch the rounded tip to form two tiny scallops. Flatten their edges and hollow on the inside with a ball tool. Shape the column over the fleshy part of the fingertip and allow to dry completely.

Roll a tiny piece of paste into a ball, approximately 2 mm ($\frac{1}{16}$ in.) in diameter, and attach to the front point of the column. Use a knife and divide this ball across the middle to form two "lips". Paint reddish-brown dots over the surface of the hollow.

Roll out a piece of paste to an approximate thickness of 1 mm ($\frac{1}{25}$ in.). Use the appropriate cutter and cut out (see *fig. 10* and *plate 20*). Cut at 1 mm ($\frac{1}{5}$ in.) intervals around the lower round edge of the trumpet and ruffle using a No. 32 Anger tool (a round toothpick will also serve the purpose).

Place the trumpet on the palm of the hand and rub the rounded edges with a modelling tool until fine and slightly transparent. Roll just inside these edges with the ball of the modelling tool to cup slightly. Leave on a rounded wooden block to obtain the correct curve (these blocks are designed for making orchids and are obtainable from cake-decorating shops). If you do not have one, curve the trumpet over a piece of rounded tin or puffed-up acrylic cottonwool.

Leave to dry completely.

Make gum paste with a little piece of modelling paste and egg white and attach to the base of the trumpet. Fix the column to this and smooth excess paste away with a fine brush. (The column fits neatly inside the trumpet.)

Roll out another piece of paste about 1 mm ($\frac{1}{25}$ in.) thick and cut out the sepals with the three-pointed cutter. Press a dried husk of maize along the length of the sepals to create veins. Lie the sepals on the palm of the hand and mould with a ball tool to thin the edge. The centre remains intact as the flower has a waxy appearance. The point of the top sepal should be modelled rounder and wider than the other two. Pinch this top point slightly to form a cup and roll lightly with a modelling tool.

Place in an individual polystyrene apple container and allow to dry. Prick a hole in the centre while still wet.

Cut out a second similar shape, but slice the top sepal to form two petals. Thin the edges with a ball tool as previously described. Again, make veins on the surface with a maize husk.

Fig. 10
Templates for making the *Cymbidium* (the small one is used to cut out the trumpet)

Mix a tiny ball of paste approximately 2 mm ($\frac{1}{16}$ in.) in diameter with a little egg white. Place this gum in the centre of the sepals which should still be slightly pliable.

Attach the petals to the sepals with the points upwards to form a well-balanced five-petaled shape. Curl the tips of the petals slightly forward and press the sides together lightly at the base to narrow and round them somewhat. Lift slightly by supporting them with a small piece of foam rubber or acrylic cottonwool. Prick a hole in the centre.

Place another small piece of paste mixed with egg white in the centre of the petals and pull the stem of the trumpet through so that the base is attached firmly to the petals. Smooth the excess paste away against the base of the trumpet, and support it with a piece of foam or cottonwool to prevent it sagging onto the petals. Place in a polystyrene container on top of a spice bottle, with the stem hanging into it. Leave to dry completely.

When dry, carefully lift off the bottle and paint the front edge of the trumpet with maroon to form marks typical to the *Cymbidium*. Leave to dry and then dust the whole flower with chalk to obtain a natural likeness.

Roll a piece of yellow modelling paste into a sausage with a diameter of about 3 mm ($\frac{1}{8}$ in.). The length must be about two-thirds that of the lip of the trumpet, with pointed ends. Lie a needle or pin lengthways across this sausage and press down to form two "lips". Roll the needle slightly to hollow. This forms the pollinium. Attach with egg white to the throat of the trumpet.

Poorman's orchid

This pretty little orchid can be made in different colours such as red, pale mauve, pale pink, yellow and orange.

To make the trumpet, roll out a piece of modelling paste so that the upper third is about twice as thick as the lower two-thirds. Refer to *fig. 11* and cut out pattern A. (The measurements in the book correspond to the natural size of the orchid.) Make sure that the leg with the rounded tip is cut out of the thicker third of the paste.

Press the other four legs with the fingers to flatten and lengthen them slightly, then use the ball tool to make them thinner. Make fine cuts on the tips of these little legs and ruffle slightly. Form them into tube-like petals by turning the sides down with a pair of tweezers. Use a toothpick and spread the ruffled edges out like a fan (see *plate 20*).

Pinch the paste just below the two vertical petals with the thumb and index finger or a pair of tweezers to form a "waist" with two outstretched arms and two legs – note that the legs should be parted slightly more than in the original cut-out position.

Insert a length of covered No. 26 florist's wire into the remaining rounded leg, with the tip of the wire protruding just above the two outstretched arms. Hold this section of the trumpet between the two index fingers and roll to and fro to enclose the wire by about 20 mm ($\frac{3}{4}$ in.), tapering towards the end.

Use the sharp tip of a modelling tool and lift the paste slightly between the two vertical petals at the base of the wire. Press the tool down to make a slight hollow.

Curve the stem slightly, close to the trumpet, then leave to dry.

Roll a second piece of paste out thinly, and cut out a shape with five petals with cutter B. Press all the edges with the fingers to thin them and mould lightly on the inside with a ball tool, taking care to retain the original shape of the petals. Turn upside down, place the ball of a modelling tool on the back of the top petal and ball slightly to let the petal curl over. Turn right side up and ball the other four petals in the same way. Use a pin or a veiner and draw the vein from the base to the tip across the middle of each of the five petals. Handle carefully and put aside.

Make a very small ball of paste, approximately 1 mm ($\frac{1}{25}$ in.) in diameter, wet with egg white and place in the centre of these petals. Make a hole right through all the layers and wet with egg white again. Push the stem of the trumpet through this hole, taking care that about two-thirds of the paste casing around the wire comes out at the bottom. Remember that the trumpet must be completely dry. Smooth the excess paste from the ball against the upper third of the casing.

Put the stem down flat on a piece of polystyrene and support the flower with pieces of

Fig. 11
Templates for the poorman's orchid

43

foam rubber to retain the shape of the orchid. Allow to dry completely.

Pipe two dots on either side of the indentation at the base of the two vertical "arms" of the trumpet with a No. 1 writing tube and bright yellow royal icing. Pipe a third and slightly elongated nodule between them a little lower down.

Finally, paint a white dot on the little tip protruding above the indentation and the three yellow markings.

This orchid can be used on its own or in an arrangement with larger orchids.

Moth orchid

This is one of the most difficult but most rewarding orchids to make.

The trumpet is made first. Cut a piece of No. 24 florist's wire into a length of about 100 mm (4 in.) and cover it with florist's tape as described under the *Cymbidium*. Bend the tip of this wire around the fleshy part of the tip of the index finger so that it forms a semicircle from the one end of the nail to the other end (it should have a diameter of about 15 mm [$\frac{5}{8}$ in.]).

Mould a ball of white modelling paste (about 4 mm [$\frac{1}{8}$ in.] in diameter) around the wire semicircle, forming a little "lip" or projection on the bend between the semicircle and the length of the stem (see *plate 21*). Allow to dry.

Roll out a piece of paste to a thickness of about 1 mm ($\frac{1}{25}$ in.) and cut it out with the appropriate cutter (see *fig. 12*) to obtain a trumpet pattern. Ball the elongated sharp tip of the trumpet to thin it out. Make an incision lengthways down the centre of the elongated part of the trumpet as shown on the photograph (see example 2 in the

Plate 21
The moth orchid

second row). Roll each "feeler" to and fro between the thumb and index finger, and roll around a toothpick to curl.

Pinch the back of the trumpet from the base of the feelers to just below the two side petals. This will form a vein in the front and make the sides turn slightly inwards.

Use a ball tool and thin out the two petals at either side of the centre point to enlarge them. Place on the palm of the hand and ball slightly in the centre to cup each petal.

Leave the small straight portion intact, but brush egg white from the tip to the middle of the trumpet between the two side petals. Attach the prepared hook. Arrange the petals and feelers to shape the trumpet. Place in one of the hollows of an ice-ball tray (diameter: 20 mm [$\frac{3}{4}$ in.]) and leave to dry. This will ensure that the trumpet will hold its shape.

Make a ball of yellow modelling paste, about 4 mm ($\frac{1}{8}$ in.) in diameter. Pinch on one side between two fingers to form a triangle, and make an incision with a knife on the top flat side to form two "lips" that are slightly parted. Cut away the sharp tip of the triangle with a pair of scissors, brush with egg white and attach inside the trumpet at the base of the paste-covered hook.

Roll a piece of white paste until thin and transparent. Cut two petals out of it (see centre diagram in *fig. 12*). Please note, they should be mirror images of each other, in other words first use the one side of the cutter, turn over and use the other side. Thin these petals out with a roller, especially around the edges to make them very transparent. Vein by pressing the stem-leaf of a violet onto them (an artificial rubber leaf may also be used for this purpose). Place on acrylic

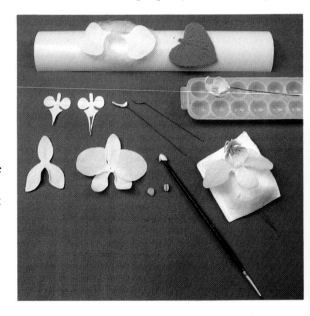

cottonwool over a rolling pin or on the round part of a piece of corrugated fibreglass. Take care that the petals do not curl up, but remain stretched out like the wings of a moth. Leave to dry thoroughly.

Next cut out the sepals with a third cutter (see end diagram in *fig. 12*). Vein each sepal with a piece of dried husk of maize as described for the *Cymbidium*. Use a ball tool and roll the back of the top sepal just above its base to cup slightly. Turn over and cup the tip of the top sepal (in the front) in the same way. Repeat this step to curl the edges and tips of the last two sepals.

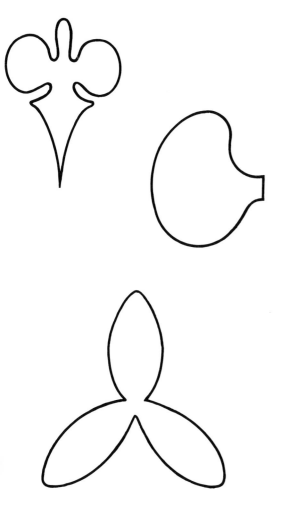

Cut out an individual container from a polystyrene fruit tray and turn upside down. Place the sepals against it, with the largest portion resting flat against the side of the container – just the two bottom tips will curl up slightly.

Cover a very tiny ball of paste with egg white and press this "gum" in the centre where the sepals meet. Attach the petals (see example 2 in the bottom row of *plate 21*). Press another piece of modelling paste over the join and brush with egg white. Prick a hole right through all the layers, including the polystyrene, and push the stem with the trumpet attached to the top through this hole. Pull tightly against the petals and into the paste. Work the excess paste neatly away with a brush. Leave to dry.

Roll a small piece of white paste on the palm of your hand to form a teardrop. The wider part of the teardrop should be about 5 mm ($\frac{1}{4}$ in.) in diameter. Use a small pair of scissors and halve the drop from the sharp tip to about 5 mm ($\frac{1}{4}$ in.) from the rounded head. Stick the back of a paintbrush into the head between the two halves. Cut the left half into a small V-shaped lip. Then roll the shaft to and fro on the right half to hollow. Cut a piece off the latter so that it will be about 10 mm ($\frac{3}{8}$ in.) long from its end to the rounded tip of the head (the distance between the point of the V and the rounded tip of the head is about 7 mm [$\frac{1}{4}$ in.]). Fit this little "hood" over the protruding tip at the base of the trumpet (attach with egg white). Smooth the paste neatly with the brush to bind the component parts together.

Allow to dry thoroughly and paint three dotted maroon lines from the base towards the outer edges of the left and right petals of the trumpet. The centre line should be slightly longer than the other two. Paint little dots in the same colour on the pollinium and draw lines across the little stem of the trumpet.

Dust the inner third of the trumpet around the pollinium with yellow chalk and colour the protruding node with rose pink.

Agapanthus

This species carries magnificent umbels of blue or white flowers and has long, smooth strap-shaped leaves. A single head can consist of up to 200 blooms. The stems are smooth and vary from 600 mm (24 in.) to 1 200 mm (48 in.) in length.

The instructions that follow are for making buds and blooms as these, not the umbels, are used for cake decorating.

Making the bud
You require a ball of white modelling paste, about 8 mm ($\frac{3}{8}$ in.) in diameter, and a length of wire (gauge 26).

Shape the paste into a teardrop over one end of the wire. It should be about 30 mm ($1\frac{1}{4}$ in.) long and 7 mm ($\frac{1}{4}$ in.) wide across the widest part.

Pinch the bulge so that the "teardrop" is pointed at the top (see *fig. 13*).

Use a scalpel or a sharp knife to make five incisions down the length of the bud. This marks the base of the petals.

Fig. 12
Templates to make the moth orchid (these as well as the previous two sets are not available in the shops and must be made specially)

45

Paint the tip and the base pale green.

Making the bloom

To start off with, you need a length of 26 gauge wire, six white stamens (17 mm [⅝ in.] to 22 mm [⅞ in.] in length, plus an additional 10 mm [⅜ in.] to allow for taping down) and a pistil, 27 mm (1$\frac{1}{16}$ in.) plus 10 mm (⅜ in.) long (to make the pistil, merely cut the anther off a seventh stamen).

Paint the anthers pale ochre.

Tape the stamens and pistil to the wire and bend them at an angle of 45°, curving their tips back and upwards as shown in *fig. 14A*.

Form a ball of white paste into a Mexican hat shape (the crown should not be more than 8 mm [⅜ in.] high). Roll out the "rim" thinly and cut out, using a template or cutter made according to the measurements in *fig. 15* (see also *fig. 14B*).

Place the flower, face down, on the palm of your hand and roll out the edges of the petals with a ball tool, thinning them but not changing their shape.

Turn over and cup each petal with the ball tool.

Push a 10 mm (⅜ in.) dowel stick, sharpened like a pencil, into the tube of the flower to hollow it out. Before removing the dowel, bend the petals down towards it to form a trumpet-shaped flower (see *fig. 14C*).

Make incisions from the corners where the petals meet nearly to the base of the tube (see *fig. 14D*).

Using a veining tool or a hat-pin, draw lines up the centre of each petal from base to tip to form the midribs or principal veins (see *fig. 14E*).

Leave the flower hanging over the dowel stick

Fig. 13
Making an agapanthus bud

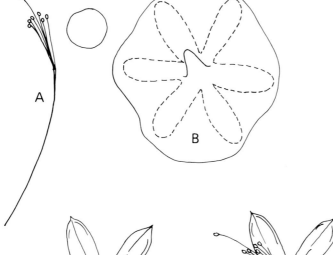

Fig. 14
Making an agapanthus bloom

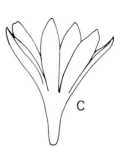

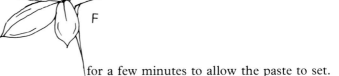

for a few minutes to allow the paste to set.

Insert the stamens and pistil by pushing the wire right through the centre of the tube. Secure at the base with egg white. (They should be placed to one side in the flower, with their tips curled back – see *fig. 14F*.)

When completely dry, dust the heart of the flower yellow-green using powder colouring. Dust the tips of the petals and the base of the tube outside.

Agapanthus blooms can be used either on their own or combined with other flowers such as small roses, carnations and gypsophila. They are

Fig. 15
Template for agapanthus blooms

particularly effective in corsages or bridal bouquets (see *plate 22*).

Peruvian lily *(Alstroemeria aurantiaca)*
These showy, irregularly shaped flowers vary in colour from bright orange to various shades of red, depending on variety or cultivar. A single flower consists of six perianth segments, that is three large and three smaller petals arranged around six stamens and a pistil with a three-part stigma.

Making the pistil
Cover a piece of 32 gauge wire, about 50 mm (2 in.) in length, with a quarter width of white tape. (You could use fuse wire instead.) Cut off the tape 20 mm ($\frac{3}{4}$ in.) above the end of the covered wire and divide this lengthways into three equal strips (see *fig. 16A and fig. 16B*).

Twist each strip between the thumb and forefinger to form three "feelers". Cut each strip back to about 3 mm ($\frac{1}{8}$ in.) long and curve it downwards (see *fig. 16C*).

Paint the whole pistil pink, using vegetable colouring (see note under stamens below).

Making the stamens
Use artificial stamens of the same length as that used for the pistil and attach a tiny ball of grey paste (about 1 mm [$\frac{1}{25}$ in.] in diameter) to one end. Make six.

Paint the stamens pink using vegetable colouring (note that adjustments are necessary when

varieties or cultivars other than shown in *plate 23* are made).

Tape the pistil and stamens to a length of 26 gauge wire, ensuring that the completed pistil is about 35 mm ($1\frac{3}{8}$ in.) and the stamens 30 mm ($1\frac{3}{4}$ in.) long (see *fig. 16D*).

Making the petals
Roll a ball of white paste into a sausage shape (the colour will have to be adjusted according to variety or cultivar) (see *fig. 17A*).

Flatten the paste with a roller, first to the one side and then to the other, leaving a small ridge at the base in the middle of the paste (see *fig. 17B*).

Cut out a narrow petal (see *fig. 20* on page 49 for size and shape of template) and thin the edges with a ball tool (see *fig. 17C*).

Turn the petal over and draw a short vein, about 5 mm ($\frac{1}{4}$ in.) long, from the tip down the centre. Turn it over again and pinch the tip of the petal lightly to emphasise the newly formed vein (see *fig. 17D*). Cup the area left and right of this, at the back, using a ball tool.

Apply egg white to one end of a piece of 32 gauge wire (fuse wire could also be used) and insert it about 10 mm ($\frac{3}{8}$ in.) deep in the base of the petal (see *fig. 17E*). Secure firmly.

Curve the tip of the petal slightly backwards and pinch the base at the back to form a small groove in front (see *fig. 17F*).

Place the petal over the back of a teaspoon to maintain the curved shape and allow to dry completely.

Make two more petals.

Follow the first two steps of these instructions and cut out the larger petal (see *fig. 21* on page 49 for a template; see also *fig. 18A and fig. 18B*). Thin the edges with a ball tool.

Plate 22
Buds, half-open, and open blooms of the agapanthus (see white flowers)

Fig. 16
Peruvian lily: making the pistil and stamens

A B C

D

Plate 23
Peruvian lilies

47

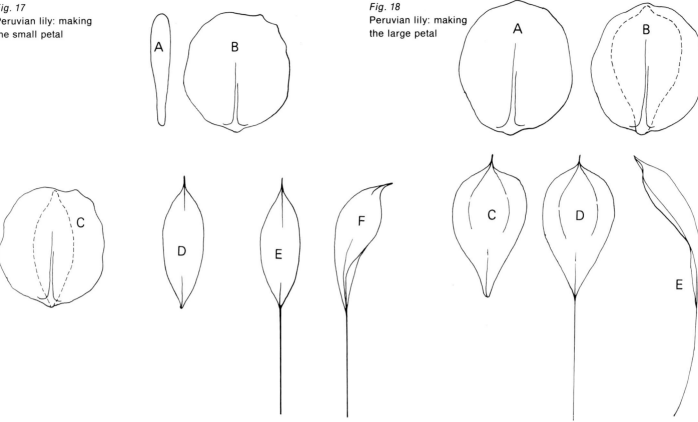

Fig. 17
Peruvian lily: making
the small petal

Fig. 18
Peruvian lily: making
the large petal

Pinch the tip of the petal at the back and, while holding it here, form an indentation down the centre of the front, using the flat end of a veining tool (see *fig. 18C*).

Turn the petal over and cup it on either side so that the edges curl back slightly.

Following the instructions given for the first set of petals, insert a piece of wire at the base (see *fig. 18D*). Pinch to form a groove.

Leave the first 10 mm ($\frac{3}{8}$ in.) of the base straight and curve the rest of the petal back at an angle (see *fig. 18E*).

Rest the top part on a piece of polyurethane and allow the petal to dry.

Make two more petals.

Dust the front and back of the narrow petals with pale pink colouring powder and shade with green powder. The tips should be a fairly bright green.

Paint elongated lengthways maroon flecks on the front over the whole petal (see *plate 23*).

Dust the larger petals in a similar fashion on the front. Turn the petal over and paint a filled-in area similar to the shape of a narrow petal, stretching over the bulge to the tip. Paint the hollow areas on either side pale pink.

Assembling the flower
Apply egg white to the base of the pistil and stamens, and attach a small ball of white paste, about 2 mm ($\frac{1}{16}$ in.) in diameter.

Tape the three smaller petals around the stamens to the stem: place two overlapping each other on one side and the remaining one opposite them (see *fig. 19A*). (This will leave two spaces, one to the left and one to the right of the single petal.)

Arrange two of the larger petals, opposite each other, in these spaces and place the third one behind the overlapping narrow petals (see *fig. 19B*). Tape to the stem.

Fig. 19
Peruvian lily: assemb-
ling the pistil, stamens
and petals

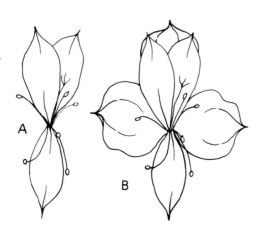

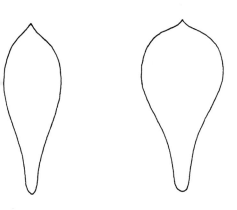

Mould a ball of green paste of about 5 mm ($\frac{1}{4}$ in.) in diameter around the base of the petals to form the ovary. Taper it at the bottom and make incisions in the thicker part to form three sections. Smooth the edges of these sections over the petals using the flat end of a veining tool (there should be no ridge).

Hint: Instead of stem leaves, use fern fronds with Peruvian lilies (see page 57 for instructions).

Azalea *(Rhododendron)*

There are a large number of *Rhododendron* species, differing in size, colour and shape of petals. Some are plain coloured throughout, while others have spots on the three upper petals. The petals vary in shape from elongated to rounded, but are always attached to a short trumpet – they are never singly arranged in a calyx.

Making the stamens and pistil
Once assembled, the pistil is about 30 mm ($1\frac{1}{4}$ in.) and the stamens 15 to 20 mm ($\frac{5}{8}$ in. to $\frac{3}{4}$ in.) in length. Add 15 mm ($\frac{5}{8}$ in.) to each to allow for taping.

Cover a piece of 24 gauge wire, about 70 mm ($2\frac{3}{4}$ in.) long, with green florist's tape and tape seven artificial stamens and a pistil to it (see *fig. 22*).

Colour the anthers light brown to pink and the stamens pink (check your model flower for colouring). Attach a small ball of yellow paste, about 2 mm ($\frac{1}{16}$ in.) in diameter, to the tip of the pistil to form the stigma. Flatten it on top and make a shallow incision across it.

Making the flower
Use paste coloured according to your model flower. To obtain a pearly shade, use white paste and paint the petals once completed. Roll a piece of paste into a cone, about 25 mm (1 in.) long and 15 mm ($\frac{5}{8}$ in.) wide across the base. Flatten the paste around the edge to form a shape similar to that of a Mexican hat (see *fig. 23A*).

Cut out the flower using a five-petal cutter about 46 mm ($1\frac{3}{4}$ in.) in diameter (see *fig. 23B*). Lift the paste and press the sharp point of an Anger tool into the centre of the flower to form a trumpet. Lay the flower, with the tool still in it, flat on the work surface and roll the tool backwards and forwards to hollow out the trumpet and flatten one petal. Lift and turn the paste anti-clockwise, rolling the tool as described, until all the petals have been flattened and widened (see *fig. 23C*).

Place the flower on the work surface with the petals face down and make 5 mm ($\frac{1}{4}$ in.) cuts up into the trumpet, in the corners where the petals meet (see *fig. 23D*).

Choose one of the petals as the main one and curl back the two petals on either side of it. Lift the flower by its trumpet and flatten the edges of the main petal so that it overlaps the other two at the base (their upper edges must lie *behind* the base edges of the main petal). Ruffle the edge of

Fig. 20 (left)
Peruvian lily: template for small petals

Fig. 21 (right)
Peruvian lily: template for large petals

Fig. 22
Azalea: making stamens and a pistil

Fig. 23
Azalea: making the flower and calyx

Fig. 24
Azalea: template for
stem leaves (make
smaller and larger
versions)

the main petal right around with an Anger tool
(see *fig. 23E*).

Flatten and ruffle the edges of the adjacent
petals in the same way, maintaining the initial
overlaps and forming new overlaps with the remaining two petals (their upper edges should lie
behind the lower edges of petals two and three)
(see *fig. 23F*).

Flatten and ruffle these petals as well, allowing
the base of the one on the right to overlap the
front of the other.

Using a veining tool, make principal veins in
the centre of each petal.

Apply egg white to the base of the stamens
where they meet the stem, insert it into the
flower and secure by moulding the paste of the
trumpet around it (see *fig. 23G*).

Making the calyx

Mould a small ball of green paste (about 5 mm
[$\frac{1}{4}$ in.] in diameter) into the shape of a Mexican
hat (see *fig. 23H*).

Cut out the calyx with a five-leaved calyx cut-
ter to be about 12 mm ($\frac{1}{2}$ in.) in diameter (see *fig.
23I*).

Thin each sepal to measure about 5 mm ($\frac{1}{4}$ in.)
and insert the sharp point of an Anger tool into
the heart of the calyx to form a trumpet. When
completed, the calyx should measure about
10 mm ($\frac{3}{8}$ in.) from tip of sepal to end of trumpet
(see *fig. 23J*).

Assembling the flower and finishing it off

Apply egg white to the inner wall of the calyx
trumpet and insert the flower, with stamens and
pistil, pushing the stem right through so that the
calyx hugs the base of the flower. Curl the sepals
back.

The azaleas in *plate 24* were made with white
paste, then coloured with pale pink powder
colouring. The edges of the petals are left white
and the shading becomes deeper towards the
heart of the flower. Shade similarly on reverse
side.

Making buds

Follow the instructions under "Making the
flower", but fold the petals over each other,
crinkling them slightly at the edges. When completed it resembles a rosebud.

Dust with powder colouring.

Add a calyx as for the flower.

Making the leaves

The leaves are dark green on top and paler green
underneath, and vary in length from 10 mm
($\frac{3}{8}$ in.) to 20 mm ($\frac{3}{4}$ in.). They are arranged in

groups around the bases of the flowers (see *plate
24*).

For detailed instructions, see page 56 under
Honeysuckle, but use *fig. 24* as a template.

Assembling a cluster of flowers

Tape together two flowers, a bud and as many
stem leaves as required.

Baby's breath *(Gypsophila paniculata)*
This delightful genus contains myriads of small
white, frothy flowers. Cake decorators often take
"poetic licence" and colour them to tone in with
the overall colour scheme of the cake.

Thin out a twig of dried baby's breath by cutting off some of the florets and sprigs.

Mix a quantity of flood icing, but apply a
count test of 8 to 9, irrespective of weather or
climatic conditions (see page 17). Colour if preferred. Cover each floret on the thinned-out twig
with this icing, using a paintbrush. Allow to dry.

You could also take the further liberty of attaching minute flowers to some of the flood icing
buds (see *plate 24*). These could be forget-me-
nots piped with royal icing and a No. 0 tube (see
page 34), flattened with the tip of a finger, or
made from modelling paste (roll out and cut out
with a 3 mm [$\frac{1}{8}$ in.] floral cutter).

Note: Only small quantities of stubble are per-
missible for show purposes.

Plate 24
An arrangement of
azaleas and baby's
breath

Broom (*Cytisus* **species**)

They have wiry green stems, studded with tiny leaves and myriads of small pea-shaped flowers.

Making buds

Cover a piece of 32 gauge wire, about 30 mm ($1\frac{1}{4}$ in.) long, with green florist's tape (you could also use fuse wire).

Mould a small ball of lemon-coloured paste into a cone. Depending on the size of bud you wish to make, it could range from 2 mm ($\frac{1}{16}$) to 10 mm ($\frac{3}{8}$ in.) in length.

Insert the covered wire into it and shape the cone to form a bud as shown in *fig. 25A*.

Making a half-open flower

Roll out a piece of lemon paste very thinly and cut out (see *fig. 28* for template; see also *fig. 25B*). Place, face down, on the palm of your hand and pinch from tip to base to form a midrib (see *fig. 25C*).

Fold around a large bud as shown in *fig. 25D*, securing them with egg white.

Pinch the tip of the petal slightly and curl it back so that the sides gape open, exposing the bud inside (see *fig. 25E*).

Making the flower

Roll out a piece of lemon paste very thinly and cut out a petal (see *fig. 28* for template; see also *fig. 25F*).

Slit the petal down the centre from the wide end to the base, leaving about 5 mm ($\frac{1}{4}$ in.) intact (see *fig. 25G*).

Place, face upwards, on the palm of your hand and roll out with a ball tool to cup and curl the petal edge on either side (see *fig. 25H*).

Fold around a large bud, securing it with egg white at the base, being the pointed end (see *fig. 25I* for shape and position of the two parts).

Holding the flower in one hand, grip the two tips on either side of the slit and push them down towards the base to let the petal balloon around the bud. Allow to dry.

Roll and cut out a second petal (see *fig. 25J*). Place, face down, on the palm of your hand and pinch from tip to base to form a midrib (see *fig. 25K*). Roll out the paste with a ball tool on either side of the rib to cup the petal. The base is now the rounded end (see *fig. 25L*).

Apply egg white to the base of the puffed petal and attach the newly formed one as shown in *fig. 25M*. Grip at the tip and curl back, forming an angle of about 90° between the two.

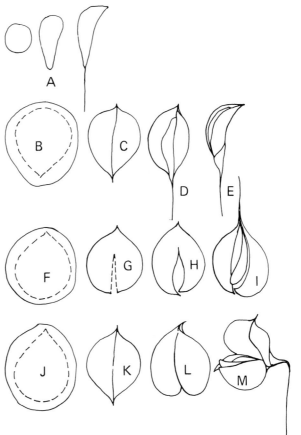

Fig. 25
Broom: making a bud, half-open and open flower

Fig. 26
Broom: making a calyx

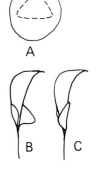

Fig. 27
Broom: assembling flowers and buds into a raceme

Making the calyx

Roll out a piece of green paste very thinly and cut out the calyx, using a small rose-petal cutter about 9 mm ($\frac{3}{8}$ in.) from tip to base (see *fig. 26A*).

Attach with egg white to the bases of buds and flowers as shown in *fig. 26B and fig. 26C*.

Assembling a spray of flowers and buds

Tape together at 5 mm ($\frac{1}{4}$ in.) intervals a collection of the smallest buds.

Attach a length of 22 gauge wire just below the last bud to serve as a stem. Tape another collection of buds to it, enlarging the buds and increasing the spaces between them as you work your way down. End with the largest bud reaching about halfway up the calyx of the bud just above it (when they are both held flush with the stem).

Add a few half-open flowers and finally some fully opened flowers (see *fig. 27*).

Note that all the flowers and buds should be arranged with their backs towards the stem (see *plate 25*).

Paint the smallest buds a greeny brown. Gradually shade to green, then green with yellow tips as the buds get bigger, ending with the largest ones left the lemon colour of the paste.

The five stamens and pistil of these flowers only become visible once they start dying. They protrude at the tip and curve back towards the stem, ranging from 6 mm ($\frac{1}{4}$ in.) to 2 mm ($\frac{1}{16}$ in.)

in length from top to bottom. The pistil measures about 10 mm ($\frac{3}{8}$ in.).

Note

The sprays could be slim, consisting of a variety of buds only, or they could be short and contain a cluster of open flowers. This allows scope as far as your arrangements are concerned.

Stem leaves are not necessary for sprays of broom.

Flame-lily *(Gloriosa superba)*

A gem of a flower consisting of six deep, rich orange or red petals, shaded yellow towards the heart. The six stamens and the pistil are borne below the corolla.

Making the stamens
Cover an 80 mm ($3\frac{1}{8}$ in.) piece of 32 gauge wire (or fuse wire) with green florist's tape. Bend the wire at a right angle 15 mm ($\frac{5}{8}$ in.) below the top end and fold it back on itself to form a "T", measuring 5 mm ($\frac{1}{4}$ in.) on either side, with the vertical length of wire (see *fig. 29A and fig. 29B*). Twist the doubled piece into one (see *fig. 29C and fig. 29D*).

Fold a ball of yellow paste, about 3 mm ($\frac{1}{8}$ in.) in diameter, over the crossbar to cover it completely (see *fig. 29E and fig. 29F*). Cut away the paste at the bottom as shown in *fig. 29G* to obtain an anther about 9 mm ($\frac{3}{8}$ in.) wide and 2 mm ($\frac{1}{16}$ in.) high. Hold the anther between your thumb and index finger and make a lengthways incision from end to end (see *fig. 29H*). Paint the slit with green colouring.

Making the pistil
Cover a 150 mm (6 in.) piece of 20 gauge wire with green florist's tape (full width) (see *fig. 29I*). Do not cut off the tape but continue rolling it into a tight spiral until about 20 mm ($\frac{3}{4}$ in.) in

length. Cut it off straight 10 mm ($\frac{3}{8}$ in.) beyond the end of the spiral and divide into three equal strips (see *fig. 29J*). Twist between your fingers to form a three-part stigma (see *fig. 29K*). Cut each back to 4 mm ($\frac{1}{8}$ in.) long (see *fig. 29L*).

Making the petals
Roll a piece of yellow paste into a cone 50 mm (2 in.) long, 8 mm ($\frac{3}{8}$ in.) wide at the base and 3 mm ($\frac{1}{8}$ in.) wide across the tip (see *fig. 29M*).

Roll out the paste to the left and the right, leaving in the centre a ridge that tapers from base to tip. Cut out a petal (see *fig. 34* on page 54 for template; see also *fig. 29O*) and draw a principal vein down its centre, over the bulge. Turn the petal over and pinch the paste from tip to base to form a midrib at the back (see *fig. 29P*).

Ruffle the edges of the petal with a toothpick or a similar small tool (see *fig. 29Q*).

Turn the petal over and run over the principal vein *in front*, using a veining tool.

Cover a 30 mm ($1\frac{1}{4}$ in.) length of wire (gauge 32) with green or white florist's tape and insert it 10 mm ($\frac{3}{8}$ in.) deep into the base of the petal. Grip the wire about 15 mm ($\frac{5}{8}$ in.) higher between your thumb and index finger and flatten the lower 5 mm ($\frac{1}{4}$ in.) of paste to form a "waist" (see *fig. 29R*).

At the base of the petal, bend the wire at right angles and then curl the petal as shown in *fig. 29S* to form a "question mark". Lay it down on its side and allow to dry. Make two more petals, then three that are slightly narrower.

Paint a red "V" on the face of each petal, the tip reaching down 15 mm ($\frac{5}{8}$ in.) above the base and the points on either side to 30 mm ($1\frac{1}{4}$ in.) above it. Leave the remainder of the surface yellow (see *fig. 30A*). Turn the petal over and paint red markings on either side of the rib. Leave a thin yellow line in the centre and an unpainted yellow crescent shape, 25 mm (1 in.) long and 5 mm ($\frac{1}{4}$ in.) wide in the centre, left and right of the vein (see *fig. 30B*).

Roll a small ball of green paste, about 2 mm ($\frac{1}{16}$ in.) in diameter, into a sausage about 1 mm ($\frac{1}{25}$ in.) in diameter and 10 mm ($\frac{3}{8}$ in.) in length. Shape the ends into points. Cut in half crosswise to obtain two small cones.

Attach one of the cones to the base of a petal with egg white. The tip should face upwards (see *fig. 31*). Pinch the paste down the centre to form a triangular sepal with a midrib. Paint the midrib with white colouring.

Paint a thin green line, about 25 mm (1 in.) long, down the rib of the petal at the back. Paint green colouring over the red layer at the base, covering an area of 5 mm ($\frac{1}{4}$ in.).

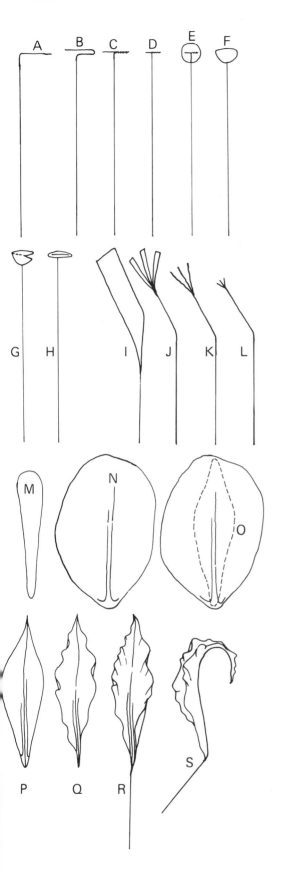

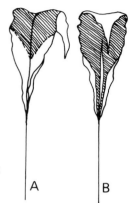

Assembling the flower

Hold the stem upright with the pistil end downwards. Tape the three narrow petals triangularly around it, about 15 mm ($\frac{5}{8}$ in.) from the corner where the pistil and stem meet. The tips of the petals should curl inwards towards the stem, as shown in *fig. 32A*.

Arrange the remaining petals in the spaces left between these petals and cut off the wires so that they end where the pistil begins.

Bend the lower 30 mm ($1\frac{1}{4}$ in.) of each stamen down and tape it to the 15 mm ($\frac{5}{8}$ in.) of stem between the bases of the flower and the pistil. Cut off the 15 mm ($\frac{5}{8}$ in.) excess wire. The stamens should be arranged in a circle, one opposite each of the petals (see *fig. 32B*).

Roll a ball of green paste, about 10 mm ($\frac{3}{8}$ in.) in diameter, into a sausage shape about 6 mm ($\frac{1}{4}$ in.) in diameter and 15 mm ($\frac{5}{8}$ in.) long. Flatten it slightly and fold it around the 15 mm ($\frac{5}{8}$ in.) section between the bases of the flower and pistil to cover all the wires. Make three equally spaced lengthways incisions to form a three-lobed ovary. Smooth the paste at the bottom down the pistil, and up and between the petals (see *fig. 32C*).

Fig. 29
Flame-lily: making stamens, a pistil and petals

Fig. 30
Flame-lily: how to paint the petals

Fig. 31
Flame-lily: finishing off a petal

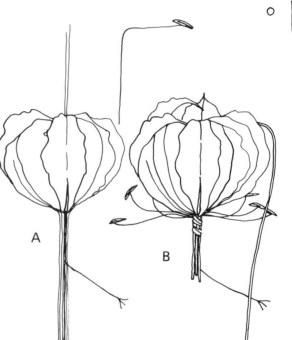

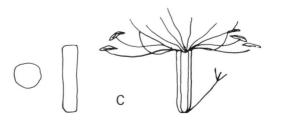

Fig. 32
Assembling a flame-lily

53

prominent one on either side of it (three in all). Exert enough pressure to ensure that three distinct ribs will be visible on the back of the leaf. Add a few less distinct lengthways veins.

prominent one on either side of it (three in all). Exert enough pressure to ensure that three distinct ribs will be visible on the back of the leaf. Add a few less distinct lengthways veins.

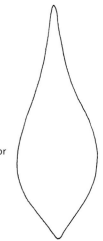

Fig. 34 (left)
Flame-lily: template
for petals

Fig. 35 (right)
Flame-lily: template for
stem leaves (make
smaller and larger
versions)

Plate 26
Flame-lilies with
broom, honeysuckle
and baby's breath

Bend the pistil up towards the flower and curve the stamens. Turn the anthers parallel. Bend the stem (still vertical) near the heart of the flower to pass between two of the petals, and curve it as shown in *plate 26*.

Making the leaves
Roll out green paste and cut out leaves (see *fig. 35* for template). Note that a fully grown leaf measures about 80 mm ($3\frac{1}{8}$ in.) by 45 mm ($1\frac{3}{4}$ in.) (across its widest part). The cross-measurement about 30 mm ($1\frac{1}{4}$ in.) from the tip can be as narrow as 15 mm ($\frac{5}{8}$ in.).

Roll out the edges lightly to curve them and curl back the point of the leaf (see *fig. 33*).

Draw a principal vein down the centre and a

Fig. 33
Flame-lily: making a
stem leaf

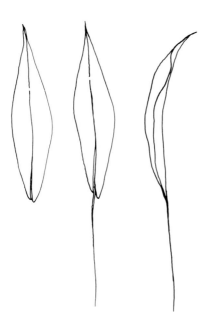

Fuchsia

Fuchsias are tubular pendant flowers, in attractive shades of red, purple and pink. They have four short petals framed by four long coloured sepals, in shades that contrast with that of the flower.

Making the stamens and pistil
Cut eight pink stamens 40 mm ($1\frac{1}{2}$ in.) long.

Pistil: attach a small ball of paste, about 1 mm ($\frac{1}{25}$ in.) in diameter in a colour corresponding with that of the species, to a stamen 50 mm (2 in.) long.

Tape the stamens and pistil to a piece of 26 gauge wire so that the stamens measure 25 mm (1 in.) and the pistil 35 mm ($1\frac{3}{8}$ in.) (see *fig. 36A*).

Making the petals
Roll out paste of the appropriate colour very thinly and cut out four petals (see *fig. 37* for template; see also *fig. 36B*).

Thin the edges with a ball tool and cup the petals.

Apply egg white to the base of each petal and place them on top of each other, fanning them out slightly at the top (see *fig. 36C*).

Assembling the flower
Mould a small ball of paste, about 2 mm ($\frac{1}{16}$ in.) in diameter in the required colour, around the base of the stamens and pistil. Cover with egg white.

Place the ball in the middle on the bottom edge of the fan of petals.

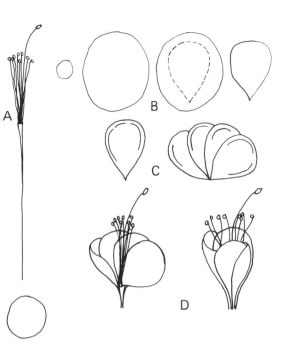

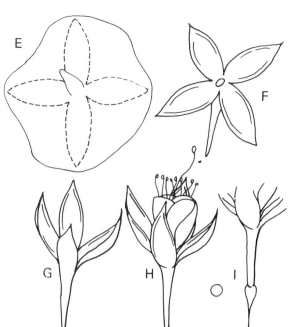

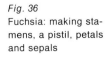
Fig. 36
Fuchsia: making stamens, a pistil, petals and sepals

Fig. 37 (below)
Fuchsia: template for petals

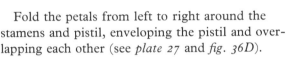

Fold the petals from left to right around the stamens and pistil, enveloping the pistil and overlapping each other (see *plate 27* and *fig. 36D*).

Allow to dry thoroughly.

Making the sepals

Shape a ball of paste in the appropriate colour to the shape of a Mexican hat (see *fig. 36E*). The length will be determined by the species you have chosen to make, but the "crown" should not measure more than 6 mm ($\frac{1}{4}$ in.) in diameter at the base.

Cut out shapes for the sepals (see *fig. 38* for template).

Thin the edges with a ball tool and cup each sepal lengthways (see *fig. 36F*).

Form a trumpet by inserting an Anger tool down the centre of the "crown".

Curl and bend the trumpet and sepals according to the fuchsia species you have chosen (see *fig. 36G*).

Assembling the flower and sepals

Apply egg white to the inner wall of the trumpet of the sepals and insert the stem with the flower. Secure (see *fig. 36H*).

Bend the sepals towards, or away from the petals to represent various stages of opening.

Taper the paste of the trumpet down the stem. Note that the shape and length varies from species to species.

Mould a small ball of green paste, about 5 mm ($\frac{1}{4}$ in.) in diameter, around the base of the trumpet to form an ovary (see *fig. 36I*).

Paint the face of the sepals to complement the petals, and shade the back and the trumpet with the same colour.

Apply a touch of green to the tips of the sepals.

Making the leaves

Roll out two pieces of green paste very thinly, one a dark green and the other a lighter shade. Cut out two leaves (see *fig. 39* for template).

Place a piece of fuse wire or 32 gauge wire on the pale green leaf and place the dark green one on top. Roll over the edges with a ball tool to secure them firmly.

Draw a principal vein down the centre on the face of the leaf, and a few small veins branching from it.

Curve and shape the leaves to look natural.

Make a number of leaves of varying sizes.

Fig. 38
Fuchsia: template for sepals

Fig. 39
Fuchsia: template for stem leaves (make smaller and larger versions)

Plate 27
A spray of fuchsias

Fig. 40
Honeysuckle: making a
flower

Honeysuckle *(Lonicera periclymenum)*

The honeysuckle has strong clasping stems and creamy flowers arranged in pairs down the stem, with two tiny leaves arranged at the base and a larger one just below them.

The flowers are irregular in shape, their petals arranged in a group of four at the top with a single one at the bottom. They are joined at the base, forming a long, narrow tube.

The age of the flowers can be determined by their colour: when the petals are white, the anthers are ripe; as the anthers fade, the petals turn yellow and the stigmas become receptive.

Tape five stamens, varying in length from 16 mm ($\frac{5}{8}$ in.) to 20 mm ($\frac{3}{4}$ in.), and a pistil (a stamen about 30 mm [$1\frac{1}{4}$ in.] long) to a piece of 26 or 28 gauge wire. The measurements refer to the length of the stamens and pistil *after* taping, so add an extra 15 mm ($\frac{5}{8}$ in.) to each.

Colour the anthers pale brown and the stigma pale green.

Bend and curve them as indicated in *fig. 40A*.

Making the flower

Mould a ball of cream or white paste, about 8 mm ($\frac{3}{8}$ in.) in diameter, into a cone 30 mm ($1\frac{1}{4}$ in.) long, 1 mm ($\frac{1}{25}$ in.) wide across the base and 5 mm ($\frac{1}{4}$ in.) wide across the tip. Cut off the bulge of the tip to obtain a flat top (see *fig. 40B*).

Cut the paste at the flat top of the cone, using a pair of scissors, to form a lip 2 mm ($\frac{1}{16}$ in.) wide, 10 mm ($\frac{3}{8}$ in.) long and 1 mm ($\frac{1}{25}$ in.) thick (see *fig. 40C*).

Hold the paste upright between your thumb and index finger, with the tip pointing downwards and the "lip" draped over your index finger. Roll out the "lip" with a ball tool, lengthening it to 20 mm ($\frac{3}{4}$ in.) (this becomes the single petal) (see *fig. 40D*).

Still holding the cone upright, drape the paste opposite the rolled out "lip" over your index finger. Work it over with the ball tool as described above, ensuring that the paste measures 20 mm ($\frac{3}{4}$ in.) in length and 10 mm ($\frac{3}{8}$ in.) across the top edge (see *fig. 40E*).

Hold the paste upright so that the first, single petal lies between your thumb and index finger. Hollow it out lengthways with a toothpick.

Draw three vertical lines, evenly spaced, over the broader petal to divide it into four. Make incisions 3 mm ($\frac{1}{8}$ in.) deep down these lines and cut the edges round to form scallops (see *fig. 40F*). Hollow out as for front petal.

Insert a toothpick into the head of the cone and hollow it out to form the tube of the flower (see *fig. 40G*).

Fig. 41
Honeysuckle: template
for stem leaves (make
smaller and larger
versions)

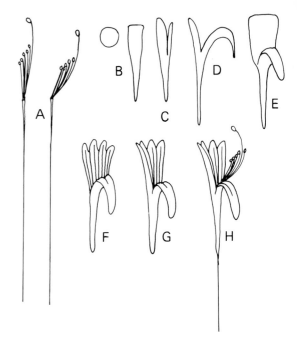

Apply egg white to the base of the stamens and pistil, and insert this into the flower, with the anthers and stigma curling up towards the group of four petals (see *plate 28* and *fig. 40H*).

The completed flower measures about 50 mm (2 in.) from the tip of the highest petal to the base of the tube.

Making the stem leaves

The leaves are almost heart-shaped (see *fig. 41* for template) and vary in length from about 8 mm × 5 mm ($\frac{3}{8}$ in. × $\frac{1}{4}$ in.) to 30 mm × 15 mm ($1\frac{1}{4}$ in. × $\frac{5}{8}$ in.).

Roll out a piece each of dark-green and pale-green paste very thinly. Cut out.

Apply egg white to a 30 mm ($1\frac{1}{4}$ in.) piece of fuse wire or 32 gauge wire and lay it down the centre of the pale green leaf. Place the dark-green leaf on top and press them together firmly.

Use a real or artificial leaf to make a vein imprint on the dark-green side.

Roll out the edges lightly and curve them to look more natural.

Making the bud

The buds vary in length from about 10 mm ($\frac{3}{8}$ in.) to approximately 30 mm ($1\frac{1}{4}$ in.). As they grow bigger, the colour changes from green to white with green tips.

Roll white paste into a cone and insert fuse wire or 32 gauge wire into it from the pointed end.

Grip the paste on either side and push it together to form an upright, slightly bowed "S" (see *plate 28*).

Making buds
Mould a "teardrop" over a stamen as described in step one under "Making the flower".

Make as many flowers and buds as required and assemble them as desired (compare *plate 29*).

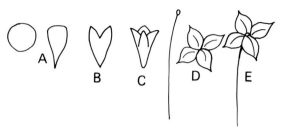

Use pale-green colouring and paint the lower 1 mm ($\frac{1}{25}$ in.) of the tubes of the buds as well as the flowers.

Assembling a spray
Tape buds to the top of a length of wire covered with green florist's tape, progressing to white and then yellow flowers, interspersed with leaves (see *plate 28*).

Lilac *(Syringa vulgaris)*
The flowers have four petals and are tubular, and the leaves are heart-shaped and smooth. Depending on the cultivar, the lilac flower may be single or double and vary in colour from white to pale yellow, mauve, purple or reddish purple. For cake-decorating purposes, they may be used individually as fillers, or arranged in sprays or clusters.

Making the flower
Mould a small ball of white paste, about 6 mm ($\frac{1}{4}$ in.) in diameter, into the shape of a teardrop, measuring about 10 mm ($\frac{3}{8}$ in.) in length (see *fig. 42A*).

Holding the bulge upwards, make an incision 5 mm ($\frac{1}{4}$ in.) deep and part the two halves. Split each into two (see *fig. 42B*) to obtain a circle of four sections. Spread evenly (see *fig. 42C*).

Holding the paste upright, thin out each section over your index finger, using the flat part of a veining tool to obtain four petals.

Pierce a hole in the heart of the flower with a pin and draw a principal vein from tip to base down the centre of each petal.

Pinch the tips of the petals lightly to make them more pointed (see *fig. 42D*).

Pull a small stamen through the hole until just its tip shows. Secure it at the base and smooth the paste (see *fig. 42E*).

Plate 28
Buds and blooms of the honeysuckle, assembled into a spray

Fig. 42
Lilac: making a flower

Plate 29
Buds and blooms of the lilac

Maidenhair fern *(Adiantum raddianum)*
The maidenhair is a graceful and delicate fern, which can be used to great effect in floral arrangements of any kind.

Strip the fronds of a dried maidenhair or asparagus fern *(Asparagus plumosus)* of their foliage.

Roll out green modelling paste thinly, until almost transparent, and cut out a multitude of little leaves (see *fig. 43* for template).

Place the fern skeleton on a board covered with wax paper (do not grease it) and clothe it with leaves. You need only exert slight pressure to make the paste stick to the network of branches.

Leave for several days to dry.

57

Fig. 43

Maidenhair fern: template for leaves

Remove very carefully from the paper with the aid of a very thin spatula.

Colour the terminal points of the leaves reddish-brown (see *plate 23* on page 47).

Tape the frond to a length of 26-gauge wire if necessary.

Note: The leaves may be frilled before attaching them, but this requires extreme patience as it is a slow, tedious process.

Nasturtium *(Tropaeolum majus)*

The flowers are showy and occur singly in leaf axils. They are made up of five sepals ending in a short or long spur, five irregularly shaped petals, eight stamens and a superior ovary.

Making the stamens

Mould a ball of green paste (about 3 mm [$\frac{1}{8}$ in.] in diameter) into a teardrop shape over one end of a length of 26-gauge wire (see *fig. 44A*).

Make three lengthways incisions in the paste to form a three-lobed ovary (see *fig. 44B*).

Cut eight stamens with very fine anthers to a length of about 20 mm ($\frac{3}{4}$ in.). Arrange these in a circle around the ovary, letting the anthers extend 7 mm ($\frac{1}{4}$ in.) beyond it (see *fig. 44C*). Tape them to the wire below the ovary and bend the stem outwards as shown in *fig. 44D*.

Paint the anthers ochre.

Hint: If stamens with very small anthers are not available, dip short lengths of thin cotton thread into egg white and then into a mixture of gelatine and colouring powder to form anthers.

Making the sepals and spur

Roll a piece of lemon-coloured paste into a ball about 12 mm ($\frac{1}{2}$ in.) in diameter and pinch to form the spur, measuring about 30 mm ($1\frac{1}{4}$ in.) lengthways and 4 mm ($\frac{1}{8}$ in.) across where it is attached to the ball (see *fig. 44E*).

Flatten the ball slightly, then mould and roll out into the shape of a Mexican hat. Cut out sepal shapes (see *fig. 45* for template; see also *fig. 44F*).

Thin the edges with a ball tool and cup the sepals slightly. Work the paste with a ball tool so that the spur forms an extension of the upper central sepal. There is a sepal to the left and the right of the latter and two opposite it.

Insert a toothpick or similar object into the spur from the end of the upper central sepal and roll it backwards and forwards to hollow it out. Curve the spur slightly outwards.

Pierce the heart of the sepals with the wire to which the stamens are attached to form a hole in the space between the base of the spur and the base of the two lower sepals (see *fig. 44G*). This ensures that when the sepals have dried and the flower been assembled, the hole will be big enough for the wire (that is the stem) to go through.

Using vegetable colouring, paint maroon lines down the centre of the three upper sepals, from the tips right down into the hollowed-out spur. Add one or more lines on either side (see *plate 30* and *fig. 44H*).

Cut out a hole in the centre of a flat piece of foam rubber. Rest the sepals on it, with the spur jutting out at the bottom. Place over a small jar or other hollow container to ensure that the sepals and spur will dry undamaged.

Making the petals

Roll out pale-yellow paste very thinly and cut out three irregularly shaped petals (see *fig. 47* for template; see also *fig. 44I*).

Thin the edges with a ball tool and draw fan-like lines from base to edge over the face of each petal (see *fig. 44J*).

Mould the short length of paste at the base of each petal into a roll to form a cauda or tail. Using a veining tool, cut the wings on either side of it at the base to form the beard of the petal (see *fig. 44K*). Bend them upwards.

Attach the petals to the sepals with egg white, covering the spaces as follows: lower left, lower right and finally lower centre, the last petal overlapping the other two on the inside (see *fig. 44L*).

Cut out two more petals, but use a different template (see *fig. 46*). Thin and frill the edges slightly with a ball tool. Vein them like the first three. Cup the lower half of each petal, face side up.

Form a cup with your thumb, index and middle finger, and drape one of the petals over your fingertips, the bulge on the back of the petal resting in the hollow. Curl the edge gently backwards. Repeat with the second petal.

Attach to the sepals with egg white, filling the upper-left and then the upper-right space.

Allow to dry thoroughly.

Paint the petals with vegetable colouring according to the markings on a specimen flower of the cultivar you wish to make. Use colouring powder for shading.

Paint green lengthways veins over the back of the sepals and colour the tips with a darker shade of green. Shade further with a trace of the colouring used for the petals.

Completing the flower

Apply egg white to a tiny ball of lemon-coloured paste, about 1 mm ($\frac{1}{25}$ in.) in diameter, and place

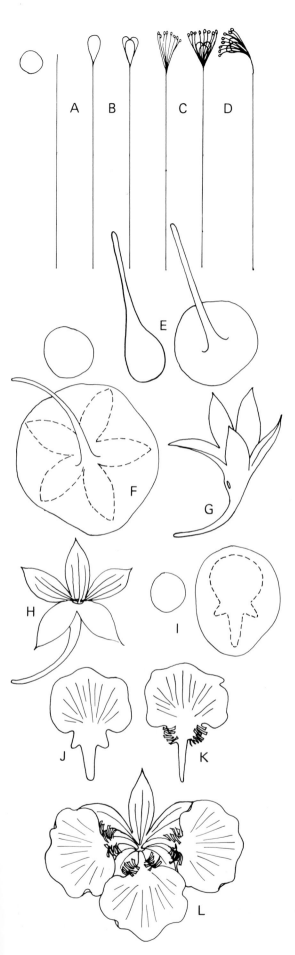

Plate 30
An arrangement of
nasturtiums

Fig. 44
Nasturtium: making a
flower

Fig. 45 (left)
Nasturtium: template
for sepals

Fig. 46 (right)
Nasturtium: template
for large petals

it over the hole made in the sepals.

Press the stem, with stamens, through it until
the ovary just rests on the ball of paste. Allow to
dry.

Making the leaves
Roll out two shades of green paste very thinly
and cut out leaves (see *fig. 48* for template). Place
a pale-green leaf in the cup of a polyurethane
apple tray.

Fold a length of wire into a "T" as described
on pages 52 to 53. Apply egg white to the crossbar and push the vertical wire through the paste
and polyurethane where the veins of the leaf
branch out.

Cut off the stem of a real leaf, flush with the
leaf. Place the leaf over the dark-green paste leaf
and press down to make veins. Arrange it over

Fig. 47
Nasturtium: template
for smaller petals

59

the leaf in the polyurethane cup and secure together. Curve the edges of the leaf slightly to make it life-like. Allow to dry.

Accentuate the veins with a lighter shade than that used for the face of the leaf. Colour the edge faintly with red.

Make as many leaves as you need, of varying sizes. Assemble with flowers as desired (see *plate 30* on page 59).

Fig. 48
Nasturtium: template for stem leaves (make larger and smaller versions)

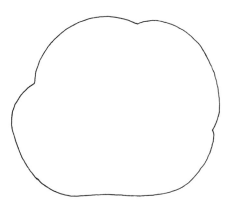

Tiger lily (*Lilium lancifolium*)
The fiery-coloured blooms of this cultivar are regular, their floral parts in units of three. There are six (three plus three), curved, pointed petals with maroon spots, the same ratio of anthers and an ovary made up of six divisions. The ovary is about 15 mm ($\frac{5}{8}$ in.) long and is found at the base of an orange-coloured pistil about 45 mm (1$\frac{3}{4}$ in.) long. If an anther were turned flush against the stamen, the length of these two parts would be equal to that of the pistil plus the ovary: about 60 mm (about 2$\frac{3}{8}$ in.)

Plate 31
An arrangement of tiger lilies and shoots of the variegated periwinkle

Making the stamens (six)
Cut a piece of 26 or 28 gauge wire 120 mm (4$\frac{3}{4}$ in.) long and cover it with white florist's tape. Measure off 70 mm (2$\frac{3}{4}$ in.) and bend the remaining 50 mm (2 in.) at a right angle (see *fig. 49A*).

Fold the 50 mm (2 in.) section back on itself so that the tip extends 10 mm ($\frac{3}{8}$ in.) beyond the angle (see *fig. 49B*). Twist the doubled section tightly to form a "T" (see *fig. 49C*).

Cut off enough wire on either side to obtain a crossbar 8 mm ($\frac{3}{8}$ in.) wide (see *fig. 49D*) and turn down the tips slightly.

Colour it orange.

Roll sufficient brown modelling paste into a ball about 3 mm (about $\frac{1}{8}$ in.) in diameter, flattening it into an oval, and fold it around the

crossbar to cover it completely. Cut away the excess paste at the bottom to obtain an anther about 2 mm ($\frac{1}{16}$ in.) by 10 mm ($\frac{3}{8}$ in.). Hold it between your thumb and index finger, and slit it across the top from end to end (see *fig. 49E* and *fig. 49F*). Paint the anther with egg white and dip it in brown colouring powder to give it a velvety finish.

Making the pistil
Cut a piece of 20 gauge wire 150 mm (6 in.) long and roll orange-coloured paste around the upper 45 mm (1$\frac{3}{4}$ in.) (see *fig. 49G*). Mould the paste into a cone 3 mm ($\frac{1}{8}$ in.) in diameter at the base and 4 mm ($\frac{1}{8}$ in.) in diameter at the top. Cut this cone to obtain a clover shape and pinch the paste to form three little lobes (see *fig. 49H*). Flatten the pistil across the top and make 5 mm ($\frac{1}{4}$ in.) incisions between the lobes (see *fig. 49I*).

Paint the tips of the lobes brown, drawing a continuous line about 2 mm ($\frac{1}{16}$ in.) long down the centre of each.

Making the ovary
Roll six pieces of green paste into little sausage shapes, 15 mm ($\frac{5}{8}$ in.) in length and 1 mm ($\frac{1}{25}$ in.) in diameter (see *fig. 49J*).

Attach them around the base of the pistil, ensuring that the ovary and pistil together are not longer than 60 mm (2$\frac{3}{8}$ in.) (see *fig. 49K*).

Assembling the stamens and pistil
Bend the pistil into a soft curve to give it a natural look.

Tape the stamens just below the ovary to the wire protruding from it, placing a stamen in each of the six grooves of the ovary. (The stamens should not be longer than the pistil.) (See *fig. 49L*.)

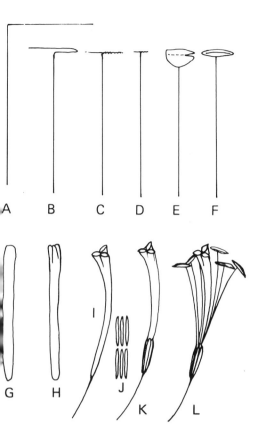

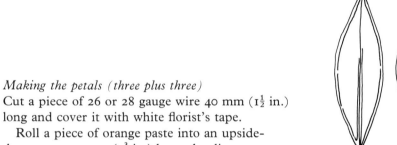

Insert a piece of 10 mm ($\frac{3}{8}$ in.) long wire in the thickened base of the petal and bend it slightly, then bend the tip of the petal backwards to form a question mark (see *fig. 50F*).

Leave until almost dry.

Dust the lower half of the petal with dark-orange powder and paint maroon spots over this section (note that the tiger lily differs from other *Lilium* species in that its petals are not spotted all

Fig. 49
Tiger lily: making and assembling the sta-mens and pistil

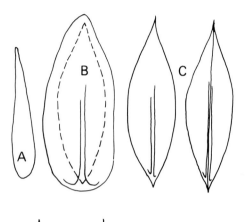

Fig. 50
Tiger lily: completing the flower

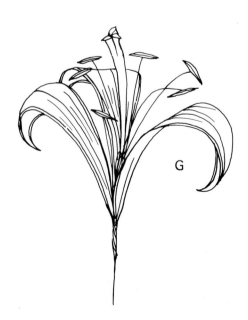

Making the petals (three plus three)

Cut a piece of 26 or 28 gauge wire 40 mm ($1\frac{1}{2}$ in.) long and cover it with white florist's tape.

Roll a piece of orange paste into an upside-down cone 70 mm ($2\frac{3}{4}$ in.) long, the diameter 10 mm ($\frac{3}{8}$ in.) at the base and 5 mm ($\frac{1}{4}$ in.) at the top (see *fig. 50A*). Flatten the cone on both sides, using a roller and leaving a 30 mm ($1\frac{1}{4}$ in.) long centre ridge, 3 mm ($\frac{1}{8}$ in.) thick at the base and tapering towards the tip.

Cut out petals as shown in *fig. 50B* (see *fig. 51 and fig. 52* for templates – make three of each). Thin the edges with a ball tool, taking care not to change the shape of the petal.

Hold the petal ridge side up and vein it down the centre. Turn it over and pinch from tip to base to form a rib (see *fig. 50C*).

Turn the petal over again and draw a line on either side of the principal vein to form two full-length lip-like structures.

Draw a thin line, about 0,5 mm ($\frac{1}{32}$ in.) from the edge, along the outline of the petal (see *fig. 50D*). Roll these strips inwards to form a cupped edge.

Draw a few lengthways veins on either side of the lip-like structures (see *fig. 50E*).

Fig. 51 (left)
Tiger lily: template for large petals

Fig. 52 (centre)
Tiger lily: template for smaller petals

Fig. 53 (right)
Tiger lily: template for stem leaves (make smaller and larger versions)

over). Dust the lower 10 mm ($\frac{3}{8}$ in.) at the base with green colouring powder.

Turn the petal over and dust the entire surface with dark-orange colouring powder. Colour the tip green.

Assembling the flower
Tape the three larger petals, evenly spaced, around the ovary, with every second stamen opposite the middle of each petal (see *fig. 50G*).

into the water and was swept away by the current. As he vanished, he cried out, "Forget me not!" Be that as it may, the flower develops from a pinkish colour when young to a deep blue, but there are also white and pink varieties (*plate 81*).

Bloom
Mould a 5 mm ($\frac{1}{4}$ in.) ball of white flower paste into the shape of a hat with a pointed crown and wide brim, and cut out bloom with a template (*fig. 54A, fig. 54B and fig. 55*).

Thin the petals with a ball tool and hollow out the trumpet with a toothpick (*fig. 54C and fig. 54D*).

Pull a fine stamen through the flower until the yellow anther rests in the throat, and set aside to dry.

Dust the edges of the petals, front and back, with blue colouring powder, leaving a white star in the centre of the flower.

Calyx
Paint the base of the flower with green vegetable colouring, as it is too small to make from paste.

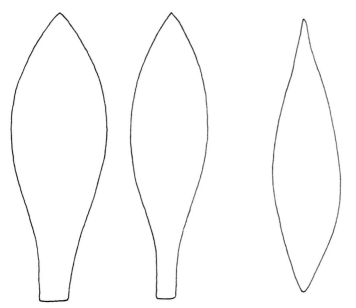

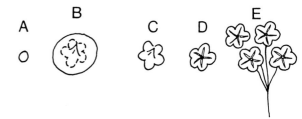

Fig. 54
Making the forget-me-not

Tape the narrower petals opposite the remaining stamens in the spaces.

Apply egg white to the stem at the base of the flower, mould a small ball of green paste around it and smooth the paste over the petals with a modelling tool (see *plate 31*).

Making the leaves
Roll out green paste and cut it into leaves (see *fig. 53* for template).

Working with a veining tool, make a principal vein down the centre and, as for the petals, draw a few lengthways secondary veins on either side of it.

Insert green florist's wire at the base, curve the leaf and allow it to dry.

Make as many as required.

Use with flowers in arrangements as desired.

Forget-me-not (*Myosotis*)
The name is said to be derived from a German legend about a knight who, while gathering flowers on the bank of a river for his beloved, fell

Bud
Mould a 3 mm ($\frac{1}{8}$ in.) ball of white flower paste into the shape of a teardrop over the anther of a fine stamen.

When dry, dust with blue colouring powder and, as for the bloom, paint a calyx at the base.

Note: Be sure to use stamens with bright-yellow anthers. Assemble the blooms and buds into clusters, or tape them together into a spray (*fig. 54E*). There are no instructions for leaves, as they are seldom used.

Purple wreath (*Petrea kohautiana*)
The petrea blooms profusely and has lovely sprays of violet-blue flowers up to 300 mm (12 in.) in length (*plate 32*). The sepals are lighter in colour than the corolla, which fades to greyish-brown and falls out before the flower dies.

Bud
Bend a small hook at one end of a piece of 32 gauge wire (*fig. 56A*). Mould a 5 mm ($\frac{1}{4}$ in.) ball

Fig. 55
Template for the forget-me-not

of violet-blue flower paste around it in the form of a teardrop, about 10 mm (⅜ in.) long and 3 mm (⅛ in.) in diameter, at the rounded tip (*fig. 56B and fig. 56C*).

Make five evenly spaced incisions halfway down the teardrop (*fig. 56D*).

Small flowers at top of spray
Make as for bud, then cut the incisions open and separate the petals. (*Alternative:* Mould some flower paste into the shape of a hat with a pointed crown and wide brim, cut it out with a template and insert a hooked wire into it – see *fig. 56E and fig. 57A.*)

Thin out and widen the petals with an Anger or small ball tool.

Secure a 1 mm (1/25 in.) ball of flower paste at the heart of the flower with egg white to represent the beginning of the corolla.

Medium-sized flowers
Follow alternative method for making small flowers, but use a larger template (*fig. 56F and fig. 57B*).

Widen and thin out the petals, then hollow out the tube of the flower with a toothpick or the point of a 3 mm (size 11) knitting needle (*fig. 56G*). Bend back the petals to prevent their spreading out like fingers.

Make a bigger bud for the corolla and place it in the centre, securing it with egg white (*fig. 56H*).

Large flowers with corolla
Follow first step for making medium-sized flowers, but use a larger template (*fig. 57C*).

Roll out a darker shade of flower paste thinly and cut it out with the template for the corolla (*fig. 57E*).

Thin it out with a ball tool and secure it with egg white in the middle of the petals (*fig. 56I*).

Hollow out the tube of the flower with the point of your Anger tool, pressing it right through the centre of the corolla.

Paint the heart an even darker shade of purple, but leave the throat white.

Old flowers without corolla
Repeat the above procedure, but use a larger template (*fig. 57D*) and leave out the corolla (it falls out as the flower gets older).

Assembling a spray
Cover a piece of 28 gauge wire with white florist's tape and tape three buds to the tip.

Tape two or three small flowers just below the buds, about 10 mm (⅜ in.) apart (the tip of the petals should reach about halfway up the flower above it).

Tape two or three of the next size flower in a similar fashion to the stem of the spray, followed

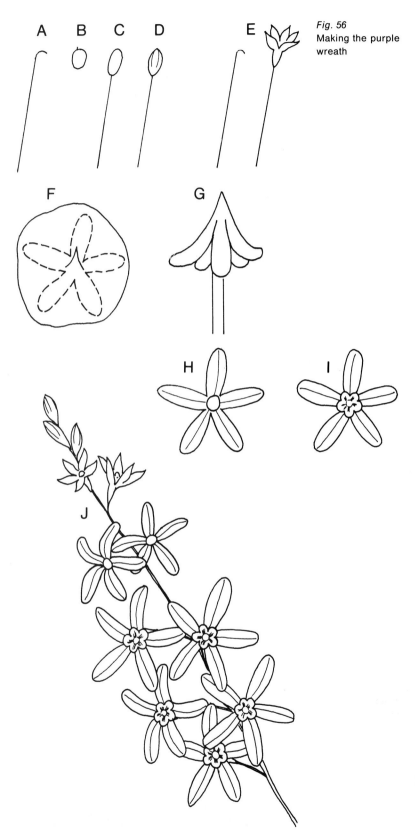

Fig. 56
Making the purple wreath

Chrysanthemum

Intermediate chrysanthemum cultivars are semi-reflexed or partially incurved, that is their petals curve back to form a globular-shaped bloom (*plate 32*). The outside petals, however, usually droop.

Small flowers

Cover a piece of 26 gauge wire with green florist's tape and bend a small hook at one end (*fig. 58A*). Mould a small piece of white flower paste into a ball 5 mm ($\frac{1}{4}$ in.) in diameter over the hook and set aside to dry completely (*fig. 58B*).

Roll out some paste thinly, cut it out (*fig. 58C and fig. 60A*) and place on a piece of sponge. Roll a small ball tool from the tip to the base of each petal to make it curve inwards (*fig. 58D*).

Brush the dried ball of flower paste with egg white and push the wire end through the centre of the group of petals. Fold them over the ball to form the first round of petals (*fig. 58E*).

Repeat the second step, using a larger template (*fig. 60B*). Secure it to the first round of petals with egg white (*fig. 58F*).

Repeat the previous step, but attach the round of petals upside down to form the drooping petals (*fig. 58G*).

Roll out some green flower paste and cut out a calyx (*fig. 58H and fig. 60C*). Secure it to the back of the flower with egg white (*fig. 58I*).

Large flowers

Cover a piece of 22 gauge wire with green florist's tape and bend a small hook at one end (*fig. 59A*). Mould a 15 mm ($\frac{5}{8}$ in.) ball of flower paste in the colour you require over the hook, forming a dome shape (*fig. 59B*).

Using a small pair of scissors and holding it at an angle, cut a row of petals from the ball as illustrated (*fig. 59C*). Open the petals out and flatten them beween the tips of your thumb and index finger.

Hold the scissors upright and cut a second row of petals into the paste, above the first row (*fig. 59D*). Do not thin these petals, but press them into shape.

Fold the outside petals over the inside ones and set the bud aside to dry completely (*fig. 59E*).

Roll out a piece of paste thinly, cut it out (*fig. 59F and fig. 62A*) and place it on a piece of sponge. Roll a small ball tool from the tip to the base of each petal to make it curve inwards (*fig. 59G*).

Brush the dried bud with egg white and push the wire end through the centre of the group of petals (*fig. 59H*). Fold them loosely over the bud and hang the bloom upside down to dry slightly.

by three or five large flowers with corollas (*fig. 56J*).

End with as many of the old flowers as you wish.

Paint the stem blueish-violet to blend with the colour of the flowers.

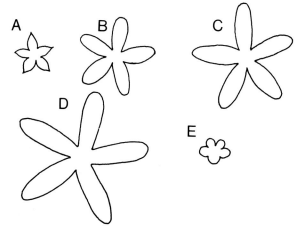

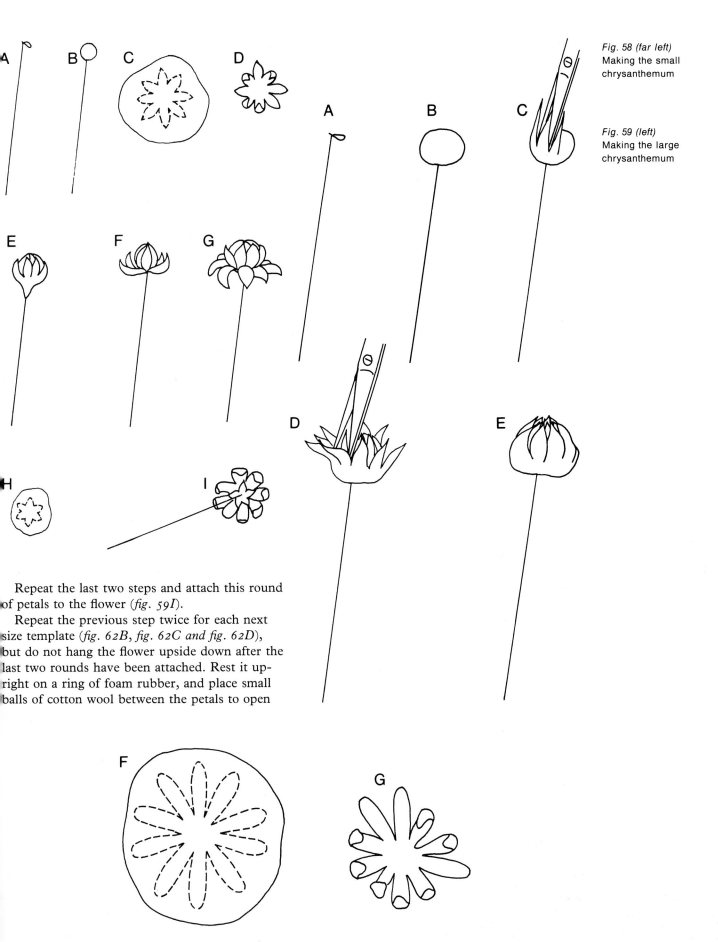

Fig. 58 (far left)
Making the small
chrysanthemum

Fig. 59 (left)
Making the large
chrysanthemum

A B C D

A B C

E F G

D E

H I

Repeat the last two steps and attach this round
of petals to the flower (*fig. 59I*).

Repeat the previous step twice for each next
size template (*fig. 62B, fig. 62C and fig. 62D*),
but do not hang the flower upside down after the
last two rounds have been attached. Rest it upright on a ring of foam rubber, and place small
balls of cotton wool between the petals to open

F G

65

Fig. 59
(continued)

H

I

them out slightly and keep them separate (*fig. 59J*). Set aside to dry completely.

Roll out a piece of green flower paste and cut out two calyxes (*fig. 62E*). Thin the sepals, leaving the bases thickened. Secure them to the back of the flower with egg white, placing the sepals of the outer calyx between the spaces of the inner ones (*fig. 59K*).

Leaves
Roll a ball of green flower paste into a sausage (*fig. 63A*) and flatten it on both sides with a roller, leaving a short ridge at the base.

Cut out a leaf with a template (*fig. 63B*) and insert a piece of 28 gauge wire into the ridge, about 10 mm (about $\frac{3}{8}$ in.) deep. Place the leaf upside down on a veiner and press it with a piece of foam rubber to make an impression of veins.

Remove the leaf from the veiner and place on crumpled-up plastic to allow it to take on the shape of a naturally curving leaf (*fig. 63C*).

Make as many as required.

Hint: A piece of foam rubber, with indentations like those in bath mats, is excellent for drying leaves.

Double gypsophila
This delightful genus contains myriads of small white, frothy flowers (*plate 33*). Cake decorators often use poetic licence and colour them to tone in with the overall colour scheme of the cake.

Roll out a piece of flower paste and cut out a round of petals (*fig. 61A*). Place it on a piece of sponge and roll out the petals with a small ball tool to cup and curl them.

Repeat previous step, but use a smaller template (*fig. 61B*) and cup the petals so that the round takes on a globular shape. Attach it to the first round with egg white.

If the flower is to be used on its own, pull a stamen through it, attaching the anther with egg white. (Make as many as required.) Alternatively, make a number of heads, set them aside to dry and attach them to real thinned-out twigs of dried gypsophila

J

K

Fig. 60
Templates for the
small chrysanthemum

A   B   C

Fig. 61
Templates for the
double gypsophila

A   B

Fig. 62 (left)
Templates for the
large chrysanthemum

Fig. 63
Making the leaves of
the chrysanthemum

Cattleya orchid

The plant bears large individual flowers (*plate 33*) and the hybrids are available in an amazing variety of colours.

Column

Bend a small hook at one end of a piece of 28 gauge wire and mould a 12 mm (½ in.) ball of flower paste into a teardrop shape (of about 20 mm [¾ in.] in length) over the hook.

Flatten the underside lengthways, widening but not lengthening it. Shape the top end into a point and make two incisions on either side. Pinch the back of the half teardrop to form a ridge from tip to base (*fig. 64A*). Set aside to dry thoroughly.

Labellum (trumpet)

Roll out a piece of paste thinly (but not transparently thin) and cut out the labellum with a template (*fig. 64B and fig. 65A*). Place the labellum over an orchid veiner and press it with a piece of foam rubber to obtain an impression.

Make the edge as frilly as possible right around by rolling an Anger tool backwards and forwards in one place (*fig. 64C*).

Plate 33
A cattleya orchid posy with double gypsophilas, maidenhair fronds and small five-petalled blossoms

Fold the labellum around the column, securing it with egg white (*fig. 64D*). Allow to set in a cone made of aluminium foil (*fig. 64E*). (*Note:* The column in a fresh flower is hardly visible and the ridged back is very close to the labellum.)

Petals

Roll a piece of flower paste into a sausage (*fig. 64F*) and flatten on either side with a roller, leaving a short ridge at the base.

Cut out a petal (*fig. 64G and fig. 65B*), place it upside down on an orchid veiner and press it with a piece of foam rubber to get an impression. Ruffle the edge with an Anger tool and pinch the upper side to form a ridge from tip to base (*fig. 64H*).

Insert a piece of 28 gauge wire in the ridge at the base of each petal and allow to dry over a slightly curved object.

Make a second petal the same way, but a mirror image.

Fig. 64
Making the cattleya orchid

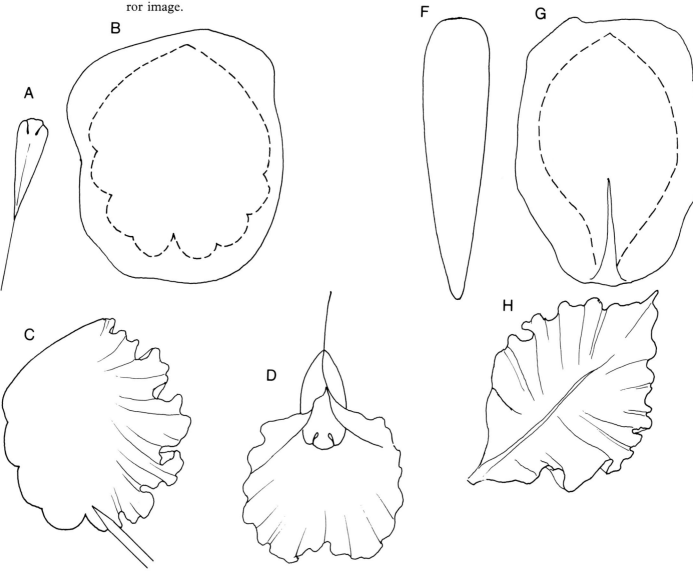

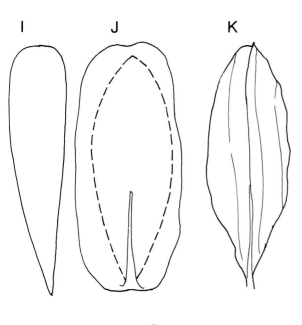

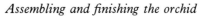

Dorsal and lateral sepals

Roll a piece of flower paste into a sausage (*fig. 64I*) and flatten on either side with a roller, leaving a short ridge at the base. Cut out a sepal, with the thin point lying on the ridge (*fig. 64J and fig. 65C*).

Using a veining tool, draw a line from tip to base down the centre of the sepal. Pinch the base all along this line, deepening the vein. Thin the edges with a ball tool and draw several more indistinct veins on the upper side of the sepal (*fig. 64K*). Insert a piece of 28 gauge wire in the ridge.

Make two more sepals.

Allow to dry with the dorsal sepal curving slightly forwards and the two lateral sepals curving slightly backwards.

Assembling and finishing the orchid

The labellum is often brightly coloured, in complete contrast to the rest of the flower, bright yellow within plain white, for instance. (Artistic licence may be used to dust and/or paint it according to the requirements of the cake.)

First tape the two petals and labellum, and then the three sepals, together. The lateral sepals hang down to the left and right underneath the labellum, and the dorsal sepal comes at the top between the two petals (*fig. 64L*).

Curve the stem and cover it with green flower paste before setting the flower aside to dry completely.

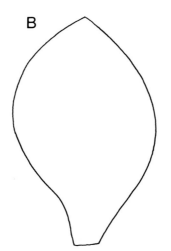

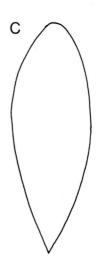

Fig. 65
Templates for the
cattleya orchid

Bank's rose (*Rosa banksiae*)

This rose is a vigorous climber and bears double white or yellow flowers (*plate 34*).

Flower

Bend a small hook at one end of a piece of 28 gauge wire (*fig. 66A*). Mould a piece of yellow flower paste into the shape of a cone, about 5 mm (¼ in.) long and 3 mm (⅛ in.) wide at the base, over the hook (*fig. 66B*). Allow to dry.

Roll out some yellow flower paste thinly and cut it out with a template (*fig. 66C*). Work the edges of each petal with a ball tool and cup them slightly (*fig. 66D*). Pull the wire supporting the cone through the centre, attaching it with egg white.

Fold alternate petals around the cone (*fig. 66E*), then fold the remaining three petals over the first three petals to form a bud (*fig. 66F*). (*Note:* If necessary, make incisions between the petals to facilitate folding.)

Using flower paste coloured a slightly paler shade of yellow, cut out a second shape. Cup the petals as described previously and repeat previous step.

Cut out a third shape in an even paler shade of yellow, cup its petals a little more than before, apply some egg white in the centre and attach it to the flower, but do not close the petals over the second row.

Hang the rose upside down until the outside petals have become firm (*fig. 66G*), moving them apart with a paintbrush whenever they close up, then set the flower aside, upright, to dry completely.

Attach a 2 mm (¹⁄₁₆ in.) ball of green flower paste to the back of the rose, using egg white.

Cut out a calyx (*fig. 66H and fig. 66I*), thin out the sepals with a ball tool and cup them slightly, then make a hollow in the centre with the ball tool.

Pull the flower stalk through the calyx and attach the sepals to the petals with egg white. Make sure that the green ball of paste is completely covered, to form the rose hip (*fig. 66J*).

These little rambler roses can be used singly or in clusters, depending on the requirements of your arrangement.

Leaves

Roll a piece of green flower paste into a sausage (*fig. 67A*) and flatten it on either side with a roller, leaving a short ridge at the base.

Cut out a long leaf (*fig. 67B*) and insert a piece of fuse wire covered with green florist's tape about 2 mm (¹⁄₁₆ in.) deep into the ridge. Place the leaf upside down on a veiner or the back of a real rose leaf and press it with a piece of foam rubber to get an impression of veins (*fig. 67C*).

Remove it from the veiner and place it on crumpled-up plastic to dry in the shape of a naturally curved leaf. (*Hint:* A piece of foam rubber with indentations like those in bath mats, is excellent for drying leaves.)

Make two pairs of smaller leaves in the same way (*fig. 67D to fig. 67I*), to obtain a set of five leaves in three different sizes. Set aside to dry.

Tape the larger pair of leaves to the big central leaf, about 2 mm (about ¹⁄₁₆ in.) from its base, followed by the smaller pair, about 6 mm (¼ in.) further down.

Dust the leaves with brown or red powdered colouring to give them a more natural appearance.

Note: When taping the fuse wire, use only an eighth of the width of green florist's tape.

Plate 34
An arrangement of bauhinias and Bank's roses

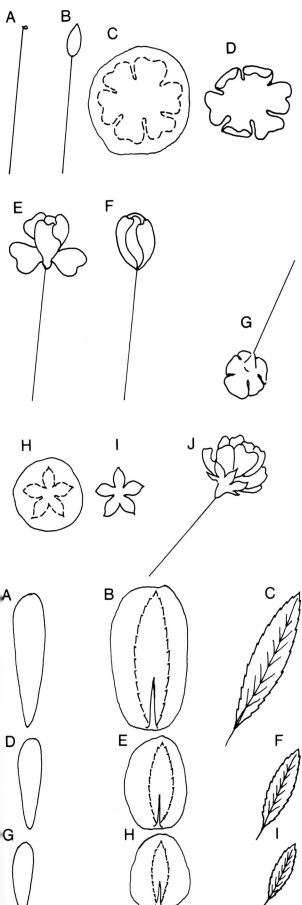

Camel's foot (*Bauhinia variegata*)

This plant is also known as the orchid tree. Its veined flowers bloom in spring just before the foliage appears. The petals vary in colour from lavender to reddish-purple and measure up to 100 mm (4 in.) across (*plate 34*). The cultivar "Candida" is smaller and has white flowers.

Stamens (five)

Use two pieces of fuse or 32 gauge wire, each measuring about 62 mm (2½ in.), and tape them with a quarter of the width of florist's tape. Form anthers by bending the top 12 mm (½ in.) of each wire horizontally and folding them back on themselves to obtain crossbars of 8 mm (⅜ in.) in length (*fig. 68A to fig. 68C*). Dip the crossbars in a pale shade of beige royal icing (*fig. 68D*). Set aside to dry.

Repeat previous step, using three pieces of wire each measuring about 72 mm (2¾ in.). When dry, curve the stamens as illustrated (*fig. 68E*).

Pistil

Use a 65 mm (2½ in.) length of wire, the same thickness as before, and bend it as illustrated (*fig. 68F*).

Mould a 6 mm (¼ in.) ball of flower paste around the middle of the wire, about 8 mm (⅜ in.) below the tip of the curve, forming a pod-shaped ovary with flat sides.

Set aside to dry, then dust with lime-green colouring powder.

Petals

Roll a piece of white flower paste, about 20 mm (¾ in.) in diameter, into a sausage (*fig. 68G*) and flatten it on either side with a roller, leaving a short ridge at the base. Cut out a petal (*fig. 68H and fig. 69A*), then thin out and ruffle the edges slightly with a ball tool. Draw a distinct principal vein down the centre, followed by subsidiary veins fanning out towards the edges. Insert a piece of 32 gauge wire about 10 mm (⅜ in.) deep into the ridge. Cut the base end into a sharp point to ensure that when it is assembled with the other petals, they will fit snugly around the stamens (*fig. 68I*). Make four petals altogether, one pair a mirror image of the other.

Repeat previous step, but use *fig. 69B* for template (see also *fig. 68J to fig. 68L*). Fold the lower edges of the petal inwards to form a shallow trumpet-like shape. Place in a cone-shaped petal former, or a cone made from aluminium foil, and set aside to dry. (Make one only.)

Fig. 66
Making the Bank's rose

Fig. 67
Making the leaves of the Bank's rose

71

Fig. 68
Making the camel's
foot (bauhinia)

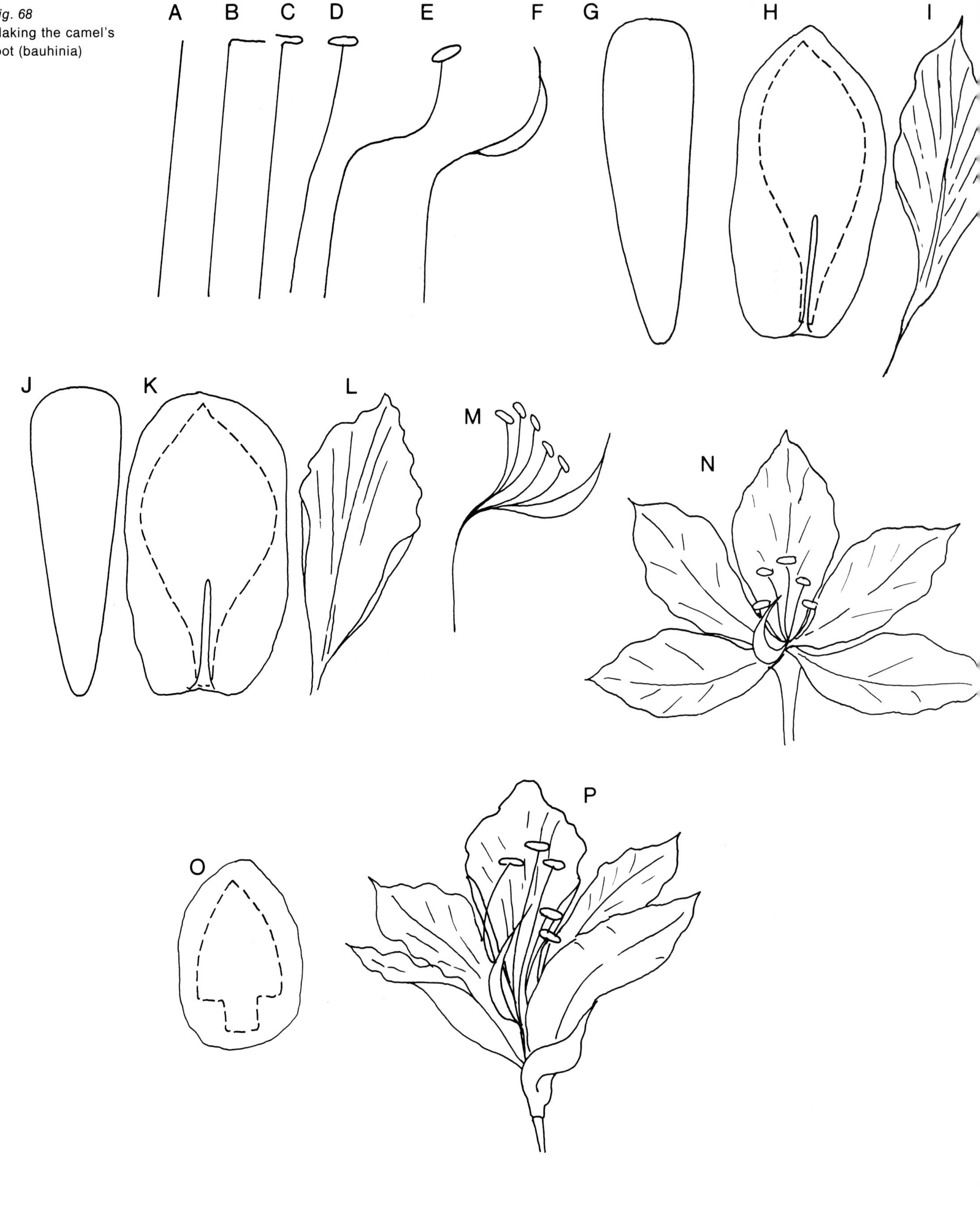

A   B   C   D   E   F   G   H   I

J   K   L   M   N

O   P

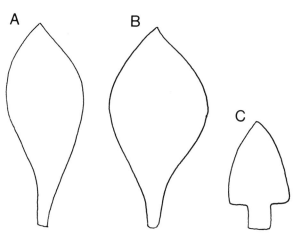

A B C

Fig. 69
Templates for the
camel's foot (bauhinia)

Assembling the flower
Tape the pistil and five stamens together as illustrated (*fig. 68M*).

Tape the centre petal to these, the stigma pointing towards its tip, followed by the remaining two pairs of petals, their bulges towards the pistil (*fig. 68N*).

Calyx
Roll out green flower paste (not too thinly) and cut out the calyx (*fig. 68O and fig. 69C*). Work with a ball tool until it forms a cupped shape. Place over your index finger and draw parallel lines with a veining tool from the tip to the base.

Attach it to the base of the petals, with the apex slightly to the right of the centre petal. Work the paste down and around the stem to cover about 15 mm ($\frac{5}{8}$ in.) (*fig. 68P*).

Dust the lower 20 mm ($\frac{3}{4}$ in.) of the centre petal with lime-green colouring powder.

Blushing-bride (*Serruria florida*)
The blushing bride bears nodding, drooping heads of white petal-like bracts, blushed with soft pink (*plate 35*). It has divided leaves, crowded towards the tips of the branches as if clasping the blooms.

Centre
Roll a piece of paste into a sausage about 15 mm ($\frac{5}{8}$ in.) in length and 5 mm ($\frac{1}{4}$ in.) in diameter. Secure with egg white to one end of a piece of 24 gauge wire covered with green florist's tape and set aside to dry (*fig. 70A*).

Using a No. 0 tube and white royal icing, pipe lengthways lines right around the sausage, making it about 10 mm ($\frac{3}{8}$ in.) in diameter. Pipe small dots on top of the sausage to resemble the tips of the stamens (*fig. 70B*).

Tease a piece of cotton wool, cut it into fine

fluff and attach it to the top of the sausage with egg white. Set aside to dry.

Roll out a piece of white flower paste very thinly and cut it into a rectangle measuring about 18 mm × 50 mm ($\frac{3}{4}$ in. × 2 in.) Cut narrow wedges from the strip, leaving a width of about 3 mm ($\frac{1}{8}$ in.) intact, to obtain a comb-like shape (*fig. 70C*).

Paint the base of the sausage with egg white and wrap the jagged strip twice around it, ensuring that the points of the second row fall in the spaces of the first row. (*Note:* The tips of the wedges must just reach the top of the sausage.) Alternatively, cut out a number of wedges and attach them individually in two rows (see *fig. 70D*). Hang upside down to dry.

When dry, draw a fine pink line lengthways down the centre of each wedge.

Paint the sides of the wedges with egg white and roll them in teased and cut cotton wool. Set aside to dry and, if necessary, cut away the excess fluff.

Dust the top of the completed centre with pale-pink colouring powder.

To make the stamens, roll a length of very pale-pink and very pale-cream cotton thread twenty times around your index and middle fingers, or use very pale-cream thread only and wind it forty times around the two fingers (*fig. 70E*). Remove and fold into a figure 8.

Secure the centre with fuse wire (*fig. 70F*), then cut the loops and attach to the base of the prepared centre with egg white. Arrange the stamens evenly around the base and tape the fuse wire to the stem with green florist's tape (*fig. 70G*). (*Note:* Use an eighth of the width of the tape to avoid making the stem too thick.) Cut the stamens about 2 mm ($\frac{1}{16}$ in.) shorter than the centre, and paint their tips with reddish-brown vegetable colouring to resemble anthers.

Perianth segments
Roll out a piece of white flower paste very thinly and cut out a set of petals (*fig. 70H*). Place it on a piece of foam rubber and cup each petal with a ball tool, then draw principal veins down their centres. Cut a hole in the centre of the round for the stem of the flower, using a No. 3 writing tube (*fig. 70I*). (*Note:* If the hole is not big enough, you'll break the petals when you insert the wire.) Turn the tips of the petals slightly outwards, and dust the centre of the round, as well as the front and the back of the petals at the base with pale lime-green colouring powder. Dust the tips of the petals very pale pink. Paint a faint pink line down the centre, front and back of each petal. Place the round of petals in a paper

73

Plate 35
Blushing brides

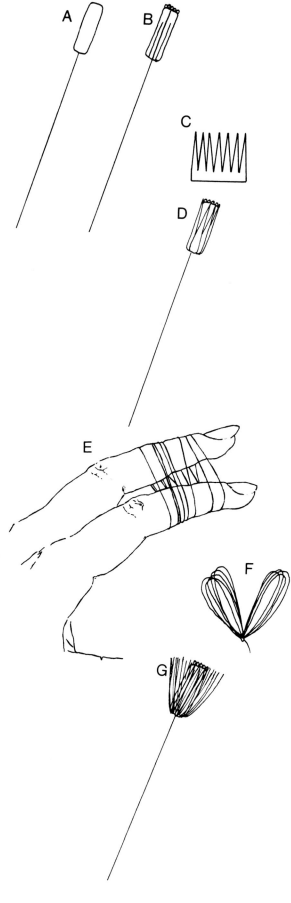

Fig. 70
Making the blushing bride

cup, about 40 mm (1½ in.) in diameter at the top and 25 mm (1 in.) at the bottom (*fig. 70J*), and allow to dry thoroughly.

Repeat previous step to obtain two similar sets of petals.

Repeat step again, but use a smaller cutter (*fig. 70K*). Make only one set of petals this size.

Roll a piece of white flower paste into a sausage. Roll it first to one and then to the other side, leaving a short ridge at the base. Cut out a petal (*fig. 70L*) and insert a short piece of fuse wire into the ridge. Secure firmly. Cup and vein the petal, and set it aside to dry. Make two more petals. Dust base of each petal, front and back, with lime-green and the tips with pale-pink colouring powder, then paint a faint pink line down their centres, front and back.

Assembling the flower
Paint the base of the stamens with egg white, pull the stem through the centre of one of the larger sets of petals, attaching the two parts (*fig. 70M*).

To separate the first round of petals from the second, wind green florist's tape round and round the stem until about 3 mm (⅛ in.) in diameter, then press the ball of tape firmly against the flower. Paint the base of the ball with egg white and attach the next matching set, arranging its petals so that they fall between the spaces of those on the first round.

Attach the third and smaller set of petals in the same way, separating them with a ball of green florist's tape.

Tape the three individual petals 1 mm (1/25 in.) apart in a spiral around the stem at the base of the flower (*fig. 70N*) (*Note:* For a specimen flower, more of the individual petals can be ad-

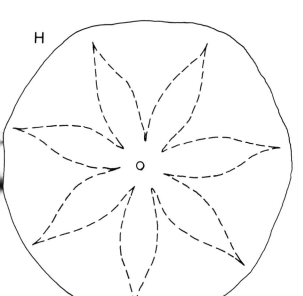

Fig. 70
(continued)

ded, making them gradually smaller and colouring them pale green, leaving out the blush of pink.)

Leaves
To make the delicate feathery leaves of the blushing bride, twist thin strips of florist's tape into spirals and then twist these together as illustrated (*fig. 70N*).

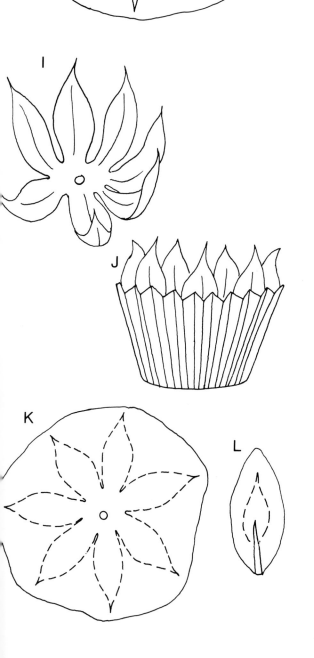

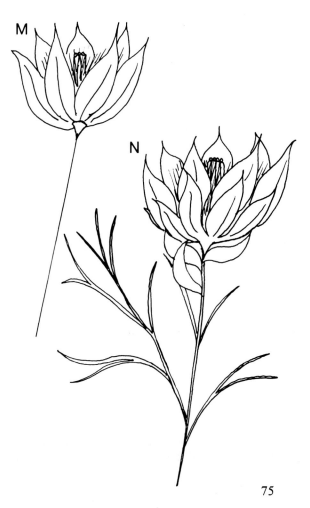

75

Make four evenly spaced slits, each about 3 mm ($\frac{1}{8}$ in.) long, around the upper edge. Cut each section to a point, thus forming the calyx of the flower (*fig. 71D and fig. 71E*). Set aside to dry.

Roll out yellow flower paste thinly and cut out four petals (*fig. 71F and fig. 72*). Thin the edges with a ball tool and draw a principal vein down the centre, followed by a network of radiating smaller veins (*fig. 71G*).

Cup the petals slightly and attach to the calyx with egg white. Set aside to dry.

Place five stamens, each about 2 mm ($\frac{1}{16}$ in.) in length, in the heart of the flower, then dust the petals with dark-yellow, brown or purple colouring powder, depending on the variety you are making.

Use the flowers singly or in groupings (*fig. 71H*).

Bud
Mould a 5 mm ($\frac{1}{4}$ in.) ball of maroon flower paste into the shape of an upside-down teardrop over the anther of a stamen. Set aside to dry (*fig. 71H*).

Note: There are no instructions for leaves as they are seldom used.

China flower (*Adenandra villosa*)
This plant develops showy terminal flowers with roundish, shiny white petals suffused with red (*plate 37*). Red glands are borne at the ends of the stamens, and the leaves and sepals are flat.

Calyx
Mould a piece of flower paste into the shape of a hat with a wide brim and a pointed crown, 10 mm high × 3 mm across ($\frac{3}{8}$ in. high × $\frac{1}{8}$ in. across) at the base, and cut out the calyx (*fig. 73A and fig. 74A*).

Thin the sepals with a ball tool and hollow out the tube with a toothpick.

Pull a piece of 28 gauge wire through the calyx and attach it with egg white (*fig. 73B and fig. 73C*). Set aside to dry.

Petals
Roll out white flower paste thinly and cut out five petals (*fig. 73D and fig. 74B*).

Stretch and thin out each petal by working it with a ball tool in the palm of your hand, then draw a principal vein down the centre from tip to base.

Attach the petals to the calyx with egg white, placing them slightly overlapping between the sepals (*fig. 73E*). Set aside to dry.

Use reddish-pink colouring powder and draw a

Plate 36
Close-up of wall-flowers on a fantasy wedding cake with mice

Wallflower (*Cheiranthus cheiri*)
Wallflowers come in a number of varieties and a wide selection of colours – white, golden brown and different shades of yellow, purple, pink and red (*plate 36*). The blooms measure about 20 mm ($\frac{3}{4}$ in.) across and are grouped together on a stem.

Bloom
Bend a small hook at one end of a piece of 32 gauge wire and mould a 5 mm ($\frac{1}{4}$ in.) ball of maroon flower paste into a sausage 10 mm × 2 mm ($\frac{3}{8}$ in. × $\frac{1}{16}$ in.) around it (*fig. 71A to fig. 71C*). Form the ovary by making an indentation about 2 mm ($\frac{1}{16}$ in.) above the base, using a pin held horizontally.

Hollow out the top part of the sausage by in-

Fig. 71
Making the wallflower

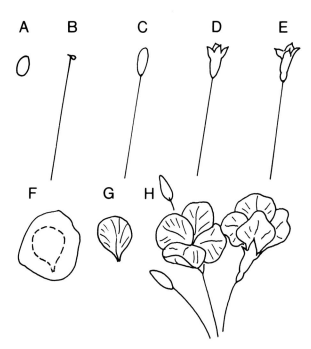

Fig. 72
Template for the wallflower

line down the centre of each petal, starting with a point at the tip and becoming wider towards the base.

Turn the flower over and dust the back of the petals and calyx with the same shade of colouring powder.

Pipe a little green royal icing in the throat of the calyx and insert eight short, red stamens in it, letting them protrude about 4 mm ($\frac{1}{8}$ in.). When dry,

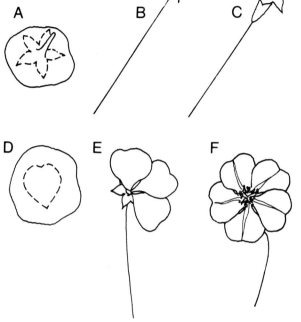

brush the tips of the stamens with egg white and dip them in a mixture of yellow colouring powder and maize-meal to form the pollen (*fig. 73F*).

Use these flowers as fillers in arrangements.

Wild iris *(Dietes grandiflora)*
The wild iris *(plate 38)* grows in large clumps and has six white perianth segments with yellow or brown markings near the base. The three central segments are mauve and contain stigmas beneath which are three stamens. The leaves are dark green, rigid and sword-shaped, and can be up to 1 m (40 in.) long.

Small perianth segments (make three)
Roll a small piece of mauve flower paste into a sausage. Flatten it with a roller, first to one and then to the other side, leaving a small ridge at the base. Cut out a perianth segment *(fig. 75A)*.

Thin the edges with a ball tool, place segment upside down on a piece of sponge and draw a central vein from tip to base. Pinch the vein on the upper side to raise it, then draw radiating subsidiary veins with an Anger tool or toothpick. Ruffle the edges slightly.

Cover a piece of fuse or 32 gauge wire with white florist's tape and insert it in the ridge. Curve the segment as illustrated *(fig. 75B)*, bending the tip slightly towards you. Set aside to dry. Make two more segments.

Tape the three segments together as in *fig. 75C*.

Using white flower paste, make a thickening about 8 mm ($\frac{3}{8}$ in.) in length around the wires at the base of the segments.

Large perianth segments (make three, plus three)
Follow first step for small perianth segments, but use a different template *(fig. 75D)* and white flower paste. Thin the edges with a ball tool

A   B

Fig. 75
Making the wild iris

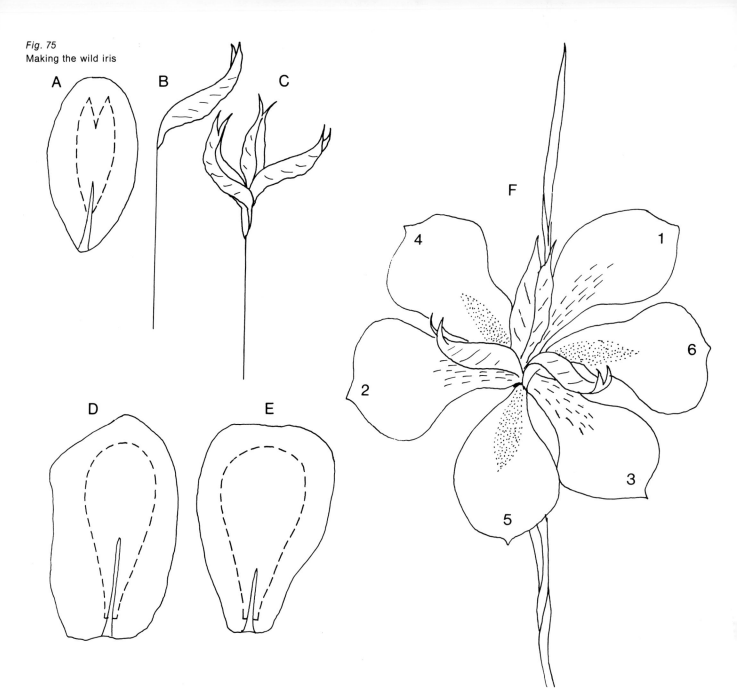

and draw lengthways veins on the top side (*plate 38*). Ruffle the edges slightly. Cover a piece of fuse or 32 gauge wire with green florist's tape and insert it in the ridge. Curve the lower 15 mm ($\frac{5}{8}$ in.) of the segment backwards and set aside to dry. Make two more segments.

Repeat previous step, using a larger template (*fig. 75E*).

When all the segments are dry, paint short dark-brown broken lines over the lower part of the smaller white segments (*Nos. 1 to 3 in fig. 75F*). Paint the lower part of the larger white segments with yellow colouring and, while still wet, sprinkle some yellow pollen (page 20) over it to create a raised effect (*Nos. 4 to 6 in fig. 75F*).

Assembling the flower

Tape the three smaller white segments, evenly spaced, around the stem just below the thickening of the mauve segments, followed by the larger white segments, filling the spaces left (*fig. 75F*).

78

Cosmos (Bidens formosa)

Cosmos are traditionally white, pink or red, (plate 39), but new cultivars in bright red and orange are now also available.

First calyx

Bend a small hook at one end of a piece of 26 gauge wire and flatten it to form a horizontal circle (fig. 76A).

Mould a piece of flower paste into the shape of a hat with a wide brim and a rounded crown, 7 mm ($\frac{1}{4}$ in.) in diameter at the base and 6 mm ($\frac{1}{4}$ in.) high.

Cut out a calyx (fig. 76B and fig. 77A) and thin the sepals with a small ball tool. Make a shallow indentation in the throat.

Dip the bent part of the wire in egg white and push the shaft through the calyx, securing the ring in the paste (fig. 76C).

Plate 39
Cosmos decorating a greeting card and pierrot on an occasional cake for Mother

Fig. 76
Making the cosmos

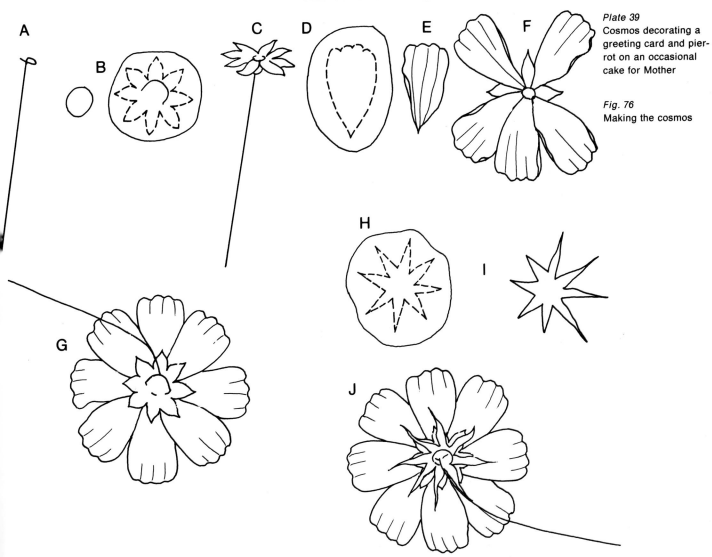

79

Fig. 76
(continued)

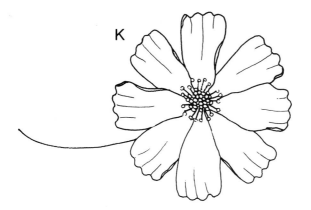

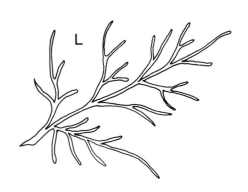

Fig. 77
Templates for the cosmos

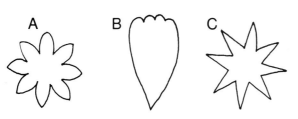

Petals

Use flower paste in the colour of the flower you wish to make and roll it out thinly. Cut out eight petals (*fig. 76D and fig. 77B*).

Thin the petals slightly with a ball tool and place them on a flat piece of foam rubber. Draw three distinct lines between the scallops from top end to base of each petal. Draw further short, fine lines down the scalloped edge with light strokes of the veining tool (*fig. 76E*).

Cup the sides of each petal with a ball tool.

Secure the petals to the calyx with egg white (*fig. 76F and fig. 76G*) and allow to dry, upright, in a hollow container to form a slightly cupped flower.

Second calyx

Roll out some flower paste thinly (a deeper shade of green than for the first calyx) and cut out a round of sepals (*fig. 76H and fig. 77C*).

Roll the tips of the sepals into thin, sharp points, curving and bending them back slightly (*fig. 76I*). Brush the centre with egg white and secure the calyx to the back of the flower (*fig. 76J*). Set aside to dry.

Centre

Using a No. 1 writing tube, pipe tiny blobs of yellow royal icing in the centre of the flower, forming a dome shape.

Insert a circle of short black stamens, about 6 mm ($\frac{1}{4}$ in.) in length, around its outside edge (*fig. 76K*).

Using a brush, place a drop of soft yellow royal icing on the tip of each stamen, then dust each with a deeper shade of colouring powder to form pollen.

Leaves

Roll out some green flower paste transparently thin to about 40 mm ($1\frac{1}{2}$ in.) wide and 70 mm ($2\frac{3}{4}$ in.) long. Place a piece of taped fuse wire in the centre, securing it with egg white.

Cover with another thin layer of paste and roll out transparently thin to both sides, amalgamating the two layers.

Cut out acute leaves as shown in *fig. 76L* and transfer the stalk with the utmost care to a piece of indented foam rubber so that the leaves can dry in a naturally curving way. (*Note:* Bend the wire slightly while the paste is still pliable to make it look more natural, and if the paste around the wire is too thick, pinch it thinner with a pair of tweezers.)

Assemble the flowers and leaves as required.

Plate 40
A close-up of the young man asking the girl for her hand in marriage

Cakes for special occasions

The first step in sugar art is to learn how to cover a cake neatly with almond paste and fondant. This has been covered in the chapter with recipes. The second step is mastering the technique of making flowers and miscellaneous decorations and doing flood work, which has been covered in the third and fourth chapters in detail.

It is, however, not enough to be efficient with modelling tools and icing tubes – one should be able to assemble the individual components to form a pleasing and well-finished whole. On the following pages you will find illustrations of examples of completed cakes for special occasions.

Plate 41
Engagement cake depicting the three stages of courting

Plate 42
Cake for an engagement or St. Valentine's day (see *fig. 81*
for pattern). Cut out hearts from plastic icing according to the
diagram and set aside to dry. Flood the cherubs and allow to
set. Make a ruffle from plastic icing to which gum tragacanth
has been added for strength. Cut out miniature hearts (keep
to decorate the board and sides of the cake) and attach the
ruffle to the outer edge of the covered cake. Place the prepared hearts on top of the cake to cover the inner edge of
the ruffle, position the cherubs and trim with paste ribbons
and flowers. Finish off the board and sides of the cake with
the miniature hearts cut from the ruffle

Plate 43
Engagement cake (see *fig. 82* for pattern). Flood the figures, paint the background with vegetable colouring and pipe royal icing flowers directly onto the cake. Attach the boy and girl, then finish off the top edge with lacework (see *fig. 150 to fig. 152* for a selection of patterns). Pipe an embroidery design around the sides of the cake (see *fig. 116 to fig. 149* for a selection of patterns) and repeat the design on the board. Trim with floral arrangements in the corners (I used roses, carnations and marguerites)

Plate 44
Close-up of engagement cake

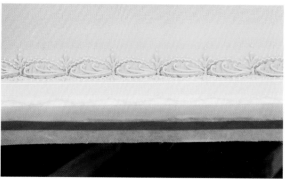

Plate 45
Cake for a kitchen tea, or a woman who loves pottering about in the kitchen (see pages 58 to 60 for detailed instructions for making nasturtiums). The strainer (shaped over a real one and the mesh piped with royal icing and a No. 00 tube), as well as the teacloth were made from modelling paste. Paint the stripes and drape the cloth while the paste is still pliable. The teapot is a round cake covered with plastic icing. The spout, handle and lid are also plastic icing, but the mixture was strengthened by the addition of a little gum tragacanth

Plate 46
Close-up of the edging around the base of the cake with nasturtiums. The piping was done in royal icing with a No. 42 Bekenal tube and a No. 0 writing tube

Plate 47
A light-blue oval wedding cake, delicately decorated with
fragile pink open roses, blossoms and anonymous flowers
(see *fig. 143* for a pattern of the border)

Plate 48
A close-up of a spray on the oval cake

85

Plate 49
A round wedding cake decorated with sprays of *Cymbidiums*, poorman's orchids, anonymous flowers, white blossoms and gypsophila (see *fig. 147* for a pattern of the border)

Plate 50
A close-up of the orchid spray on the round wedding cake

Plate 51
Two-tiered wedding
cake with blushing
brides. It consists of an
180 mm² (7 in.²) cake
combined with a 300
mm² (12 in.²) cake cut
in two, as can be seen.
It is decorated with ar-
rangements of blush-
ing brides and grey
leaves. The floral
theme is repeated in
the embroidery work
on the sides of the
cakes (*fig. 117*) and is
complemented by deli-
cate lace points (*fig.
150A*). The shell
borders were made
with a No. 42 Bekenal
tube

Plate 52
An unusual wedding
cake with collar and
sweetpeas, suitable for
a small reception (see
fig. 83 and fig. 84 for
patterns of the collars)

87

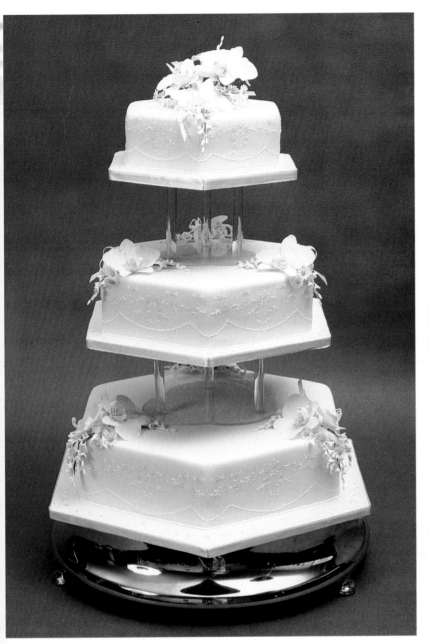

Plate 54
A white six-sided wedding cake decorated with moth orchids, hyacinths and daisies. The main colours are white and yellow, which are repeated on the border (see *fig. 142* for a pattern of the latter)

Plate 55
A close-up of the arrangement on the top layer of the six-sided cake

Plate 53 (left)
A white square wedding cake decorated with daisies of modelling paste. The border (see *fig. 146* for a pattern) is done in pale-yellow and pale-green royal icing to blend with the colour scheme of the modelled decorations

90

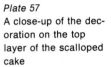

Plate 59
Wedding cake with purple wreath and chrysanthemums. Interesting features of this cake are the double lace points along the top border (*fig. 150J*) and the royal icing ribbon insertions which carry through the colour of the flowers. Figure-piped doves add a romantic touch, a theme repeated in the embroidery on the side of the cake (*fig. 116*). The top cake measures 150 mm × 150 mm (6 in. × 6 in.) and was cut from the larger cake, which measures 300 mm × 300 mm (12 in. × 12 in.)

92

Plate 60
One-tiered wedding
cake with carnations
and broom made by
Cynthia Fletcher. The
bottom edge of the
cake is finished off
with extension and
bridge work (see
pages 29 to 31) and
the board with built-up
line work (see page
28)

Plate 61
Three-tiered wedding
cake with broom,
flame-lilies and honey-
suckle finished off with
extension and bridge
work (see pages 29 to
31)

Plate 62

Filigree wedding cake with bride and arch (see *fig. 86 to fig. 94* for patterns).

Prepare the cake (it should be 200 mm [8 in.] in diameter), six-sided board, bride, platform (it is made from pastillage and consists of three steps each, about 3 mm [$\frac{1}{8}$ in.] high), filigree pieces and collar.

Use a template of the collar pattern to make markings on the cake for its positioning. Pipe stars about 5 mm ($\frac{1}{4}$ in.) high accordingly and attach the collar.

Place the platform in the middle of the cake and position the bride on it.

Assemble the vault and side panels of the arch, and once set, lift over the bride with a paintbrush. Attach to the cake with royal icing. (*Note:* The side panels of the arch have to be exactly vertical, otherwise stress from the vault will cause them to bend and snap.) Place floral arrangements in the inner scallops of the collar and then move on to the lower section of the cake.

Place six arrangements of flowers on the board opposite the sides, not the corners, of the hexagon. Make markings between them to correspond exactly to the corners of the collar on top of the cake. Pipe dots in royal icing from one corner halfway to the next along the edge of the collar; also pipe a 20 mm ($\frac{3}{4}$ in.) row of dots in the same direction on the board from the corner of the corresponding marking. Attach a prepared filigree panel. Attach a mirror image of this panel in the same way to form an archway. Repeat right around the cake. Pipe dots down all the joins of the panels and attach pendant lace pieces to the centre of the vaults of the bottom arches. The board is finished off with scalloped piping

94

Plate 63
Close-up of bride on filigree wedding cake with arches

Plate 64
Close-up of a bottom arch of the filigree wedding cake with
bride and arches

Plate 65

Wedding cake with bride and groom. This is a versatile design, as the bottom layer can be used on its own as a single-tier cake for a small wedding. The figures were made according to the Mexican method, which is not described in this book, but could also be made using moulds (page 25).

A total of 29 Bank's roses, 17 rosebuds, 75 anonymous flowers, 12 bauhinias, 20 sprays of hyacinths, 24 sprays of five-petalled blossoms and 29 miniature azaleas were used for the arrangements. (For the embroidery pattern, see *fig. 118*)

Plate 67
Fantasy wedding or anniversary cake with mice. This heart-shaped cake was decorated with extension and bridgework. Agapanthus, china flowers and wild irises were used for the floral arrangements. The heads of the mice were made using a putty mould (page 25), while their bodies and arms were moulded freehand. (*Note:* The head and arms should be at-tached as described under *Modelling and dressing figures*, pages 24 to 25). When dry, paint the bodies with a brush and very thin coloured royal icing. The cake is finished off with little hearts and musical notes. (For the lace-point pattern, see *fig. 150B*)

Plate 68
A cake in the shape of a horse shoe for a 25th wedding anniversary. The frangipani arrangement is finished off with
paste ribbons (turn to *fig. 149* for the pattern of the border)

Plate 69

Cake for a 50th wedding anniversary. Bake two rectangular cakes 150 mm × 230 mm × 20 mm (6 in. × 9 in. × $\frac{3}{4}$ in.). Cover with marzipan, then cover two short and one long side with white plastic icing; make impressions with a sterilised ruler to form pages.

Roll out coloured plastic icing for one of the covers and proceed as follows: Cut the cover according to the length and twice the width, plus 30 mm (1$\frac{1}{4}$ in.) of the pages; place on a sheet of plastic, then put the cake on top of it, to one side, so that the pages face outwards. Fold the rest of the icing over the cake with the aid of the plastic sheet, forming a rounded back for the book. Decorate with gilt embroidery which stretches over the back as well, and add the wording. Make a second book, but omit the "title".

Assemble on a board as in photograph and decorate with sprays of flowers. The embroidery finishing on the board was done with royal icing and a No. 0 Bekenal tube (see *fig. 116 to fig. 149* for a selection of patterns)

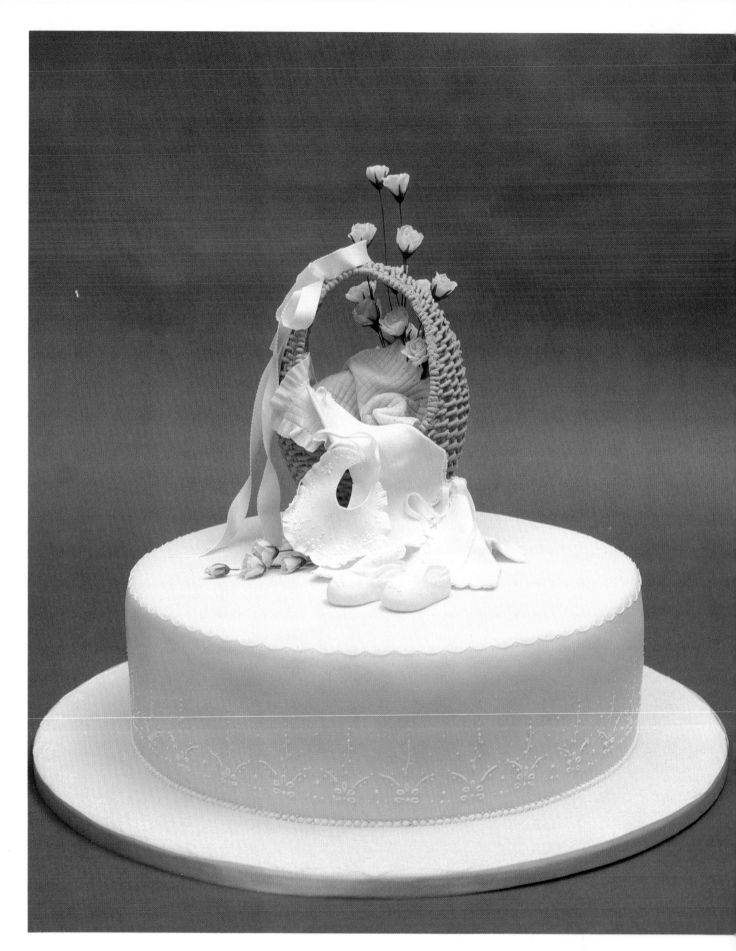

Plate 70 (opposite)
A christening cake with basket, baby blanket, bib, matinée jacket and bootees, finished off with paste ribbons, yellow Cécile Brunner roses and lacework (see *fig. 144* for border pattern)

Plate 71
For balance, rhythm and composition the central motif of this christening cake is complemented with Cécile Brunner roses, anonymous flowers, paste ribbons, cherubs and delicate blossoms

Plate 72
A close-up of the side view of the christening cake with babe

Plate 73 (top)
Cake with baby's bedroom scene. The furniture was made from pastillage and assembled with royal icing. (*fig. 95A to fig. 95K*). The rocking horse (*fig. 95L*) was cut out of flower paste rolled out to about 5 mm ($\frac{1}{4}$ in.) thick. The bear was moulded freehand, but could also be made using a plaster of Paris mould (page 25). An arrangement of roses, carnations, hyacinths and five-petalled blossoms adds colour and balance to the design, while ribbons and bibs made from flower paste lend an unusual finishing touch to the sides of the cake

Plate 74 (below)
Cake with napkin pins. Mould seven babies freehand as described on page 24. Cut the hooks of the safety pins from

flower paste (*fig. 96*) and make the wire parts with a clay gun. Attach in position and finish off the cake with miniature roses, bibs and toys

Plate 76 (opposite)
Birthday cake for a little boy (see *fig. 97 to fig. 100* for patterns). Flood the boys, as well as the tennis rackets, cricket bats and balls (the strings of the rackets were piped with royal icing and a No. 00 tube). After covering the cake, draw lines in the paste (I coloured mine antique-white) with a veining tool to mark off four sections, and pipe brown royal icing into these grooves. Paint the backgrounds with vegetable colouring and pipe royal icing flowers on the cake. Place the figures and items in position and attach with royal icing

Plate 75
Christening cake (see *fig. 85* for pattern). Flood the top collar as well as the one on the board. Trim the cake around the base with arrangements of daisies and add the baby's name, or place a filigree or pastillage cradle in the centre

Plate 77
A birthday cake for a male who has an interest in sport. The
rice-paper technique was followed here (see page 33). Note,
however, that the pattern (*fig. 101*) may also be flooded

Plate 78
A birthday cake for a bridge enthusiast (see *fig. 102* for pattern). Extra powdered gum was added to the modelling paste for the cards, book, pencil, cigarettes and ashtray, but note that the motifs on the cards were painted onto rice paper (if preferred, they may be flooded)

Plate 79
Birthday cake for a handyman (see *fig. 103* for patterns of the hammer and saw). Cover the cake and board with grained plastic icing, and make the hammer and saw from pastillage. To form shavings, roll out modelling paste very thinly and cut into equal width strips with a parsley cutter. Wind them around a wooden skewer to form coils; allow to set slightly, then remove to dry completely. Make the nails from modelling paste, using a real nail as model. Assemble on the cake as shown in the photograph, and trim with flowers and a cord made from plastic icing with a clay gun, using a round disc about 1 mm ($\frac{1}{25}$ in.) in diameter

Plate 80
The little fisherman (see *fig. 104* for a pattern and page 23 for the instructions)

Fantasy cake with fairies. The fairies were made in the same way as the figures of the children playing on the lawn opposite (*fig. 6 to fig. 8*, pages 24 to 25). They represent flowers such as the rose, bluebell, carnation and daisy. Their wings were made by dipping fine wire frames into a solution of 5 ml (1 t) gelatine powder and 10 ml (2 t) water dissolved over heat. (*Note:* When making a frame, leave a little grip by which to handle it. And when lifting it out of the gelatine, take care not to burst the bubble.) Allow it to dry upright by pressing the grip into a piece of polystyrene. The wings may be painted with food colouring when dry. The bridge was cut out of green flower paste, using a loquat leaf as template and veiner

Plate 82
Close-up of Fantasy cake with fairies

Plate 83
Children playing on the lawn. The well, the different components of the house (*fig. 105A to fig. 105T*) and the umbrella were cut from pastillage. (*Note:* The umbrella was shaped over a plastic ball.) Flower paste was used for the children's clothes, as well as to cover a wire network for the tree. (For making and dressing the figures, see *fig. 6 to fig. 8*, pages 24 to 25)

Plate 84
Close-up of Children playing on the lawn

Plate 85
Close-up of Children playing on the lawn

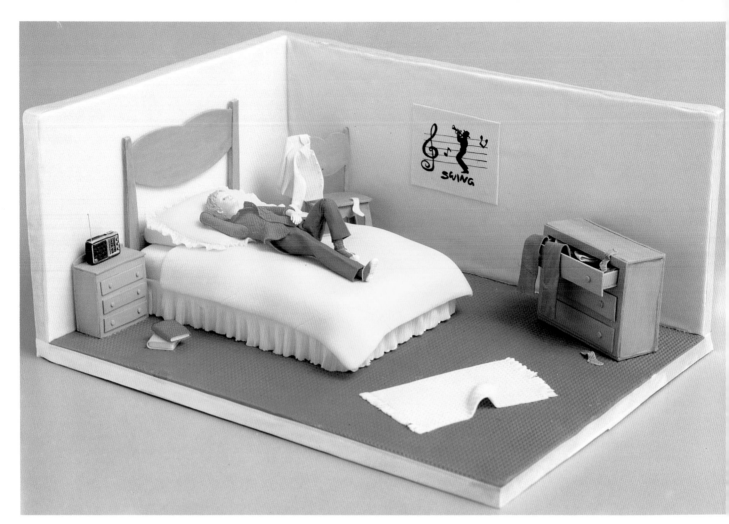

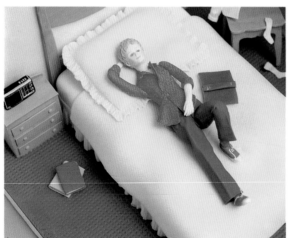

Plate 86
Teenager lounging in his room. The boy was made according to the Mexican method, which is not described in this book, but could also be made with a mould (page 25). His clothes were made from flower paste and his duvet cut from a thick layer of plastic icing so as to give a padded effect. The different components of the furniture were cut from pastillage (*fig. 106A to fig. 106R*) while the radio and books were moulded freehand. A 150 mm × 230 mm (6 in. × 9 in.) cake forms the bed

Plate 87
Close-up of Teenager lounging in his room

Plate 88
Birthday cake with Peruvian lilies

Plate 89

Cake for a girl's 21st birthday decorated with a picture in cocoa painting. White embroidery work (*fig. 121*) on a background of antique-white complements the colour of the picture. Arrangements of white daisies add a light, feminine touch, while a snail's trail finishes the bottom border. The key was made with a clay gun and flower paste, and the picture is held up by a pastillage disc. (For embroidery pattern on side of board, see *fig. 122*, and for patterns of picture and key, *fig. 107A and fig. 107B*)

Plate 90

Close-up of embroidery work on cake for a girl's 21st birthday decorated with a picture in cocoa painting

Plate 91
A 21st birthday cake for a girl. The Cécile Brunner roses, carnations, daisies and blossoms of modelling paste vary in shade from pale-pink and lilac to white. The parasol is also made of modelling paste and shaped over a rubber ball just larger than a tennis ball. For the greeting card extra powdered gum was added to the modelling paste, which was then rolled out, cut and curled. For patterns of the flood work (key) and border see *fig. 108 and fig. 148* respectively (note that the basket of the latter was converted into an umbrella)

Plate 92
Occasional cake with roses. The most striking thing about this cake is its elegant simplicity: three roses and three sets of leaves arranged on a plastic icing cloth draped over a round cake and caught with a bow to reveal the adornment of ruffles. The cloth was finished with delicate embroidery work and a picot edging, while the ruffles were made according to the Garrett frill method. (*Note:* A little CMC, gum tragacanth or Tylose should be added to the plastic icing mixture to strengthen it)

Plate 93
Occasional cake for a teenage girl. (See *fig. 109* for pattern.)
The girl was made in bas-relief (see method on page 21),
while her umbrella was cut from flower paste and draped
over half a dome shape to dry. The basket was made from
royal icing in basket weave and filled with miniature roses.
Painted-on stepping stones and clouds finish the cake, and
apple blossom arrangements the board

Plate 94
A most unusual cake for Mother on any day that is special to
her. The pierrot figurine was made according to the Mexican
technique, but you could use a porcelain doll instead, so that
Mother could keep it as a gift after the cake has been en-
joyed. The card was made from pastillage and combined
with an arrangement of white and pink cosmos. This floral
theme is repeated in the lace and embroidery work on the
side of the cake (*fig. 119 and fig. 150H* respectively)

Plate 95
A Mother's Day cake decorated with hyacinths, anonymous flowers and small *Cymbidiums*, varying in shade from deep cream to almost rust-brown. The border is unusual in the sense that it runs around the cake at an angle of 45° (see crease indication on *fig. 145*), i.e. one half should rest on the board

Plate 96
Confirmation cake (see *fig. 110* for pattern). Flood the girl
from her waist upwards (the skirt is made from modelling
paste), and also flood the window and candle. Add the skirt
after the flooded pieces have been attached in position (the
skirt is made from a crescent shape, cut from a semicircle,
to fit it around the waist). The bird is formed by figure piping
and the flowers (roses and five-petalled blossoms), ribbon
and bow are made from modelling paste. The side of the
cake is decorated with garlands of royal icing blossoms and
forget-me-nots, trimmed with flooded bows

Plate 97

Christmas, wedding or anniversary cake (see *fig. 111* for pattern of bells). Make bells from pastillage shaped over a curved object and use plastic icing for the clappers. Assemble on top of the cake with a spray of small orchids, lilac, carnations, blossoms and maidenhair fern. Embroidery done in royal icing with a No. 0 tube finishes off the sides of the cake (see *fig. 116 to fig. 149* for a selection of patterns)

Plate 98

Close-up of embroidery design and piping on board of multipurpose cake depicted in *plate 97*

Plate 99
Madonna in cocoa painting (see *fig. 112* for pattern). The roping around the plaque and the base of this Christmas cake
was done with a clay gun, while arrangements of Christmas
roses (*Helleborus niger*) and holly leaves and berries were
added for colour and balance. The floral theme is repeated
in the embroidery work on the side of the cake (*fig. 120*)

Plate 100
A round Christmas cake with a flood-work motif (see *fig. 113* for the pattern). The border is finished off with half bells, holly leaves and berries

Plate 101
Close-up of the bell-border motif (the bells are shaped in a plastic mould of modelling paste and cut in half before the paste is completely dry)

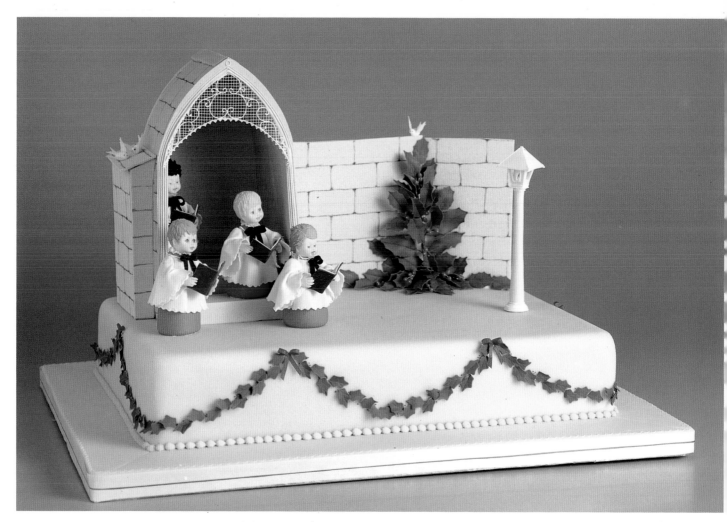

Plate 102

Christmas cake with choir boys. The arch and walls of the
church (*fig. 114A to fig.114N*) as well as the lamppost were
made from pastillage. The body of each boy consists of a red
flower paste cone over which a surplice was draped (*fig.
114O to fig. 114S*). The hands were moulded freehand, while
the heads were made with a plaster of Paris mould (page
25). The covers and pages of the hymn books were made up
with layers of green and white modelling paste (*fig. 114T*). A
holly tree (leaves on wire taped together) gives balance to
the cake, while a couple of doves add a symbolic touch of
peace. Garlands of holly leaves and berries caught by little
red bows finish the sides of the cake, and a narrow strip of
red ribbon the sides of the board

Plate 103 (right)

A Christmas cake with choir boys and a lamppost of modelling paste. The Christmas tree was made separately using
the same method as for the wings of the swan (refer to page
22), with the difference that the front is left to dry and then
the process is repeated on the other side

Fig. 78
Pattern for plaque in
bas-relief (*plate 3*)

Fig. 79

Fig. 80

125

Fig. 81
Pattern for an engage-
ment or St. Valentine's
Day cake (see *plate
42*)

126

Fig. 82
Pattern for an engage-
ment cake (see *plates
43 and 44*)

Fig. 83
This pattern should be
used with *fig. 84* (also
refer to the wedding
cake on *plate 52*)

Fig. 84
As can be seen on
plate 52 this collar fits
around the cake at the
bottom

Fig. 85
Pattern for christening
cake with storks (see
plate 75). *Note:* the
stork motifs may be re-
placed by the motif
with doves for an Eas-
ter cake

130

Fig. 86
Half collar of filigree
wedding cake with
bride

131

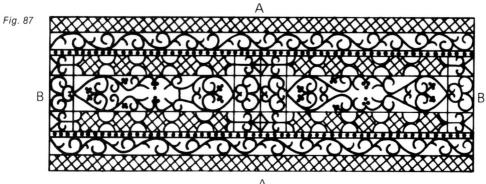

Fig. 87

Fig. 87
Vault for arch of fili-
gree wedding cake
with bride, to be piped
over an object bent at
right angles (see
plates 62 and 63)

Fig. 88
Side panel for arch of
filigree wedding cake
with bride

Fig. 89
Front view of arch over
bride

Fig. 90
Trellis pattern for vault
of filigree wedding
cake with bride (*note:*
the end piece on the
far right is positioned
in the top 90° corner of
fig. 89)

Fig. 91
Side panel for bottom
arches of filigree wed-
ding cake with bride
(*note:* a mirror image
of this pattern com-
pletes the arch)

Fig. 92
Lace decoration sus-
pended from centre
join of bottom arch of
filigree wedding cake
with bride

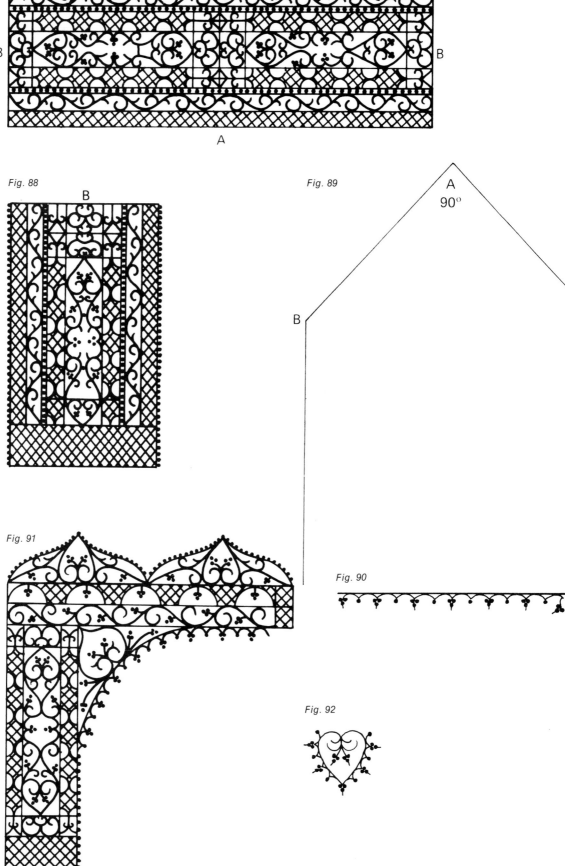

Fig. 88

Fig. 89

Fig. 90

Fig. 91

Fig. 92

132

Fig. 93
Platform for bride of
filigree wedding cake
with arch

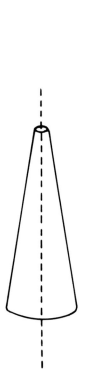

Fig. 94
Pattern of bride for filigree wedding cake
with arch

133

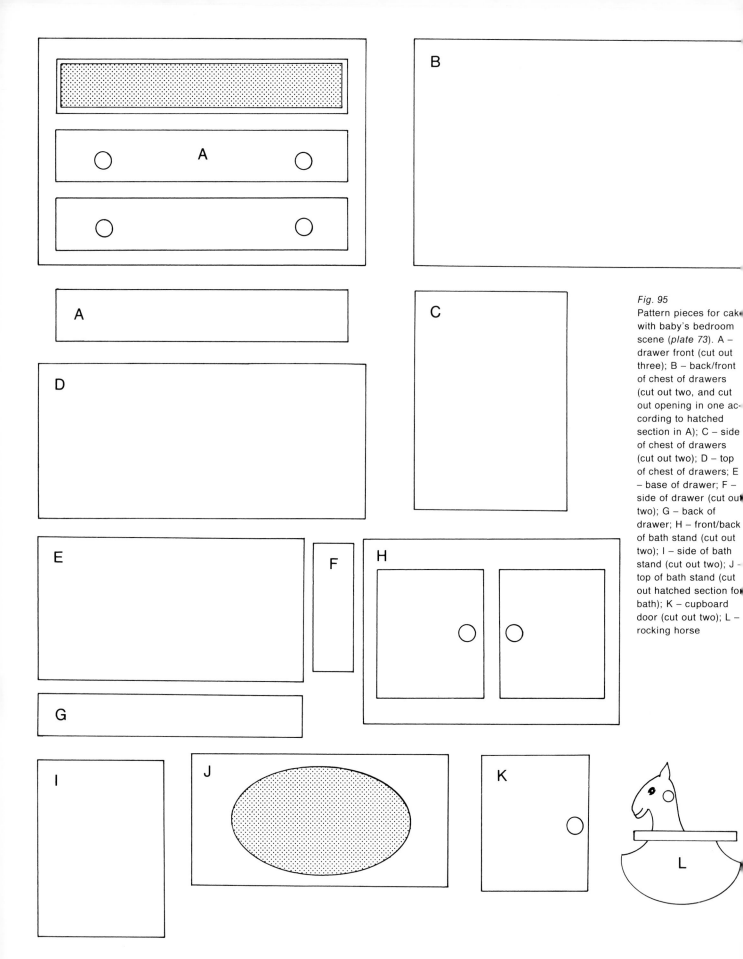

Fig. 95
Pattern pieces for cake with baby's bedroom scene (*plate 73*). A – drawer front (cut out three); B – back/front of chest of drawers (cut out two, and cut out opening in one according to hatched section in A); C – side of chest of drawers (cut out two); D – top of chest of drawers; E – base of drawer; F – side of drawer (cut out two); G – back of drawer; H – front/back of bath stand (cut out two); I – side of bath stand (cut out two); J – top of bath stand (cut out hatched section for bath); K – cupboard door (cut out two); L – rocking horse

Fig. 96
Patterns for christening cake with napkin pins (*plate 74*)

B

C

D

Fig. 97
Rugby player

Fig. 98
Tennis player

136

Fig. 99
Cricket player

Fig. 100
Soccer player (*note:* the four young sportsmen may either be used individually or grouped together, as in *plate 76*, for a little boy's birthday)

Fig. 101

Fig. 102

Fig. 103
Hammer and saw for a
handyman's birthday
cake (see *plate 79*).
The handle (brown)
and blade (grey) of the
saw are made
separately

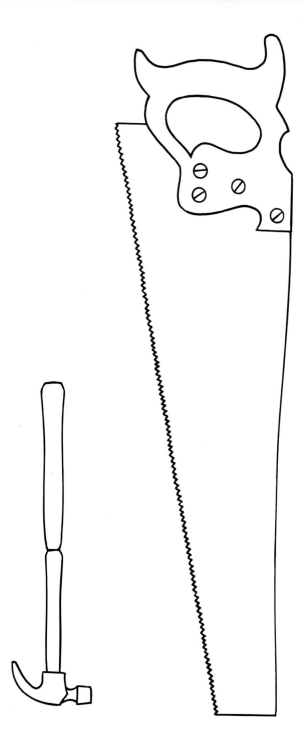

Fig. 104

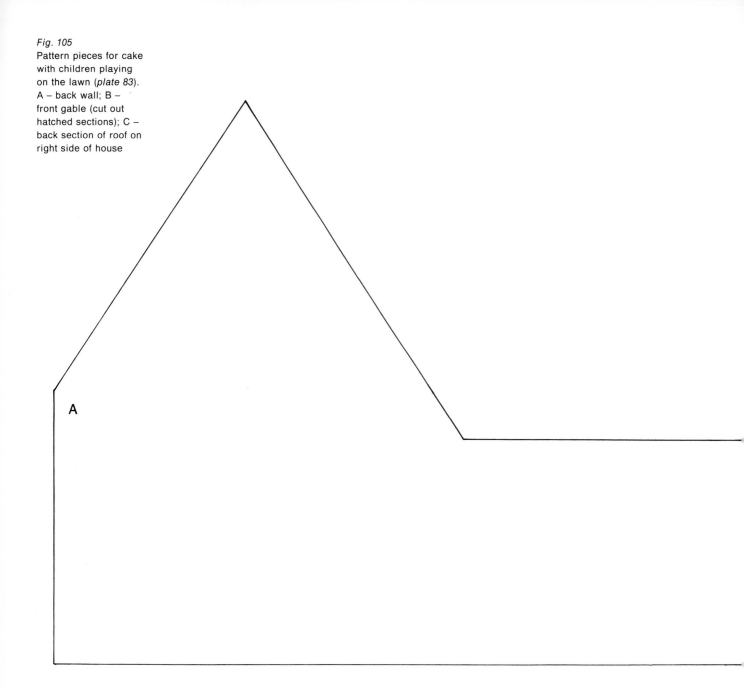

Fig. 105
Pattern pieces for cake
with children playing
on the lawn (*plate 83*).
A – back wall; B –
front gable (cut out
hatched sections); C –
back section of roof on
right side of house

A

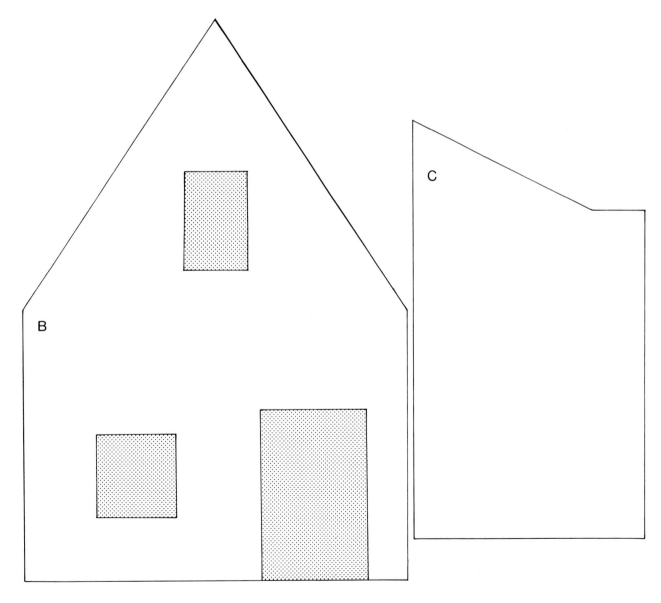

143

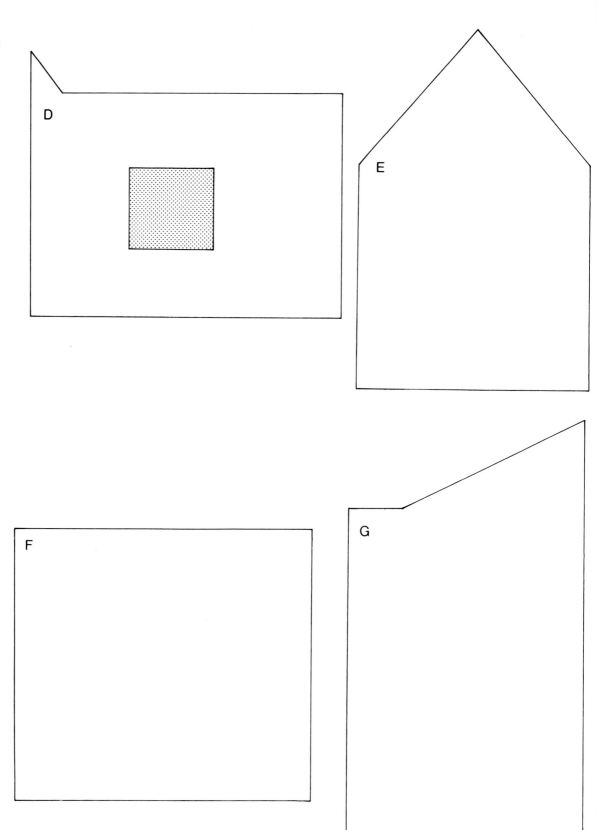

Fig. 105 (continued) D – right front wall (cut out hatched section); E – side wall on right; F – side wall on left; G – front section of roof on right side of house; H – main roof on right side of house; I – main roof on left side of house

144

H

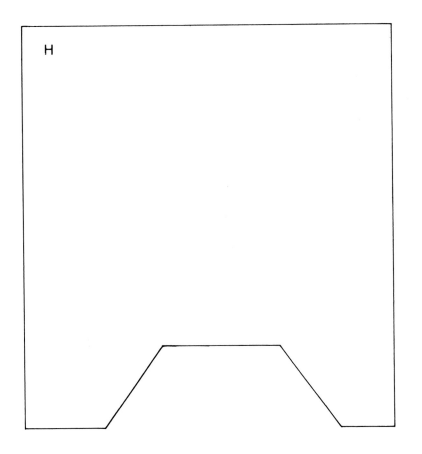

I

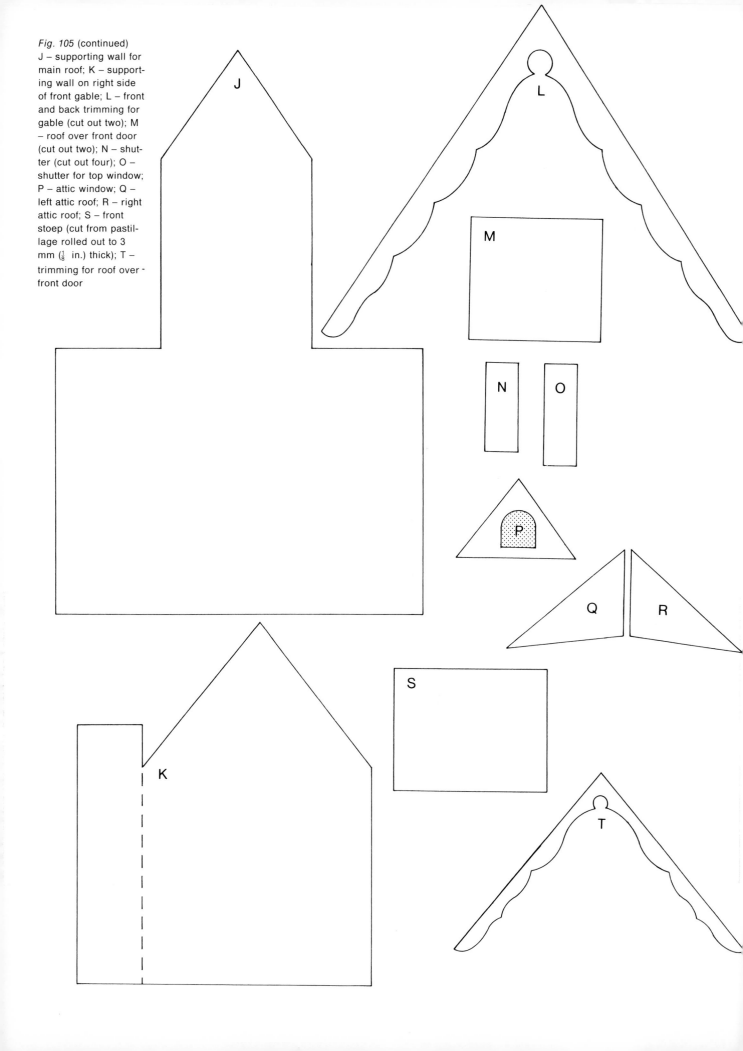

Fig. 105 (continued)
J – supporting wall for
main roof; K – support-
ing wall on right side
of front gable; L – front
and back trimming for
gable (cut out two); M
– roof over front door
(cut out two); N – shut-
ter (cut out four); O –
shutter for top window;
P – attic window; Q –
left attic roof; R – right
attic roof; S – front
stoep (cut from pastil-
lage rolled out to 3
mm ($\frac{1}{8}$ in.) thick); T –
trimming for roof over
front door

J

L

M

N   O

P

Q   R

S

K

T

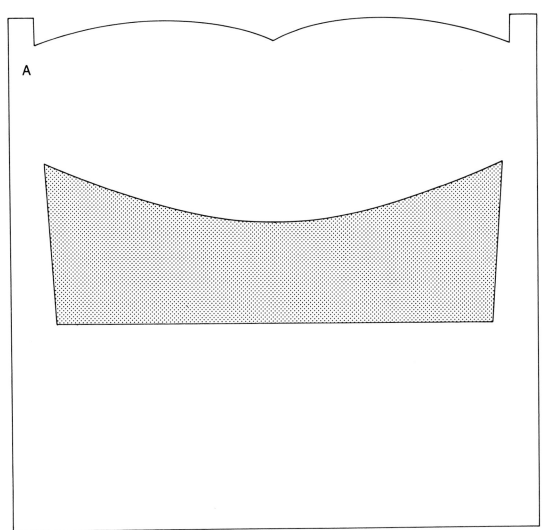

Fig. 106
Pattern pieces for cake with teenager lounging in his room (*plate 86*).
A – headboard (cut out hatched section); B – front of chest of drawers (cut out hatched section); C – back of chest of drawers

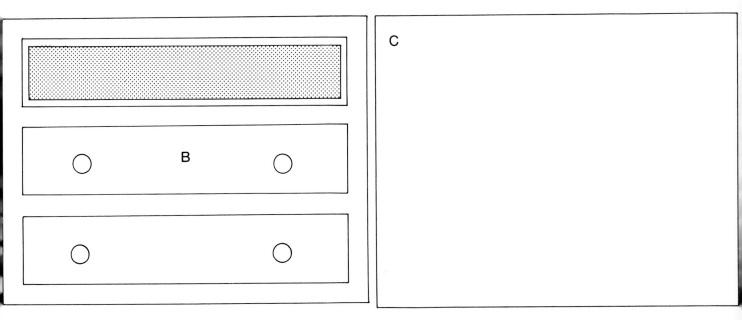

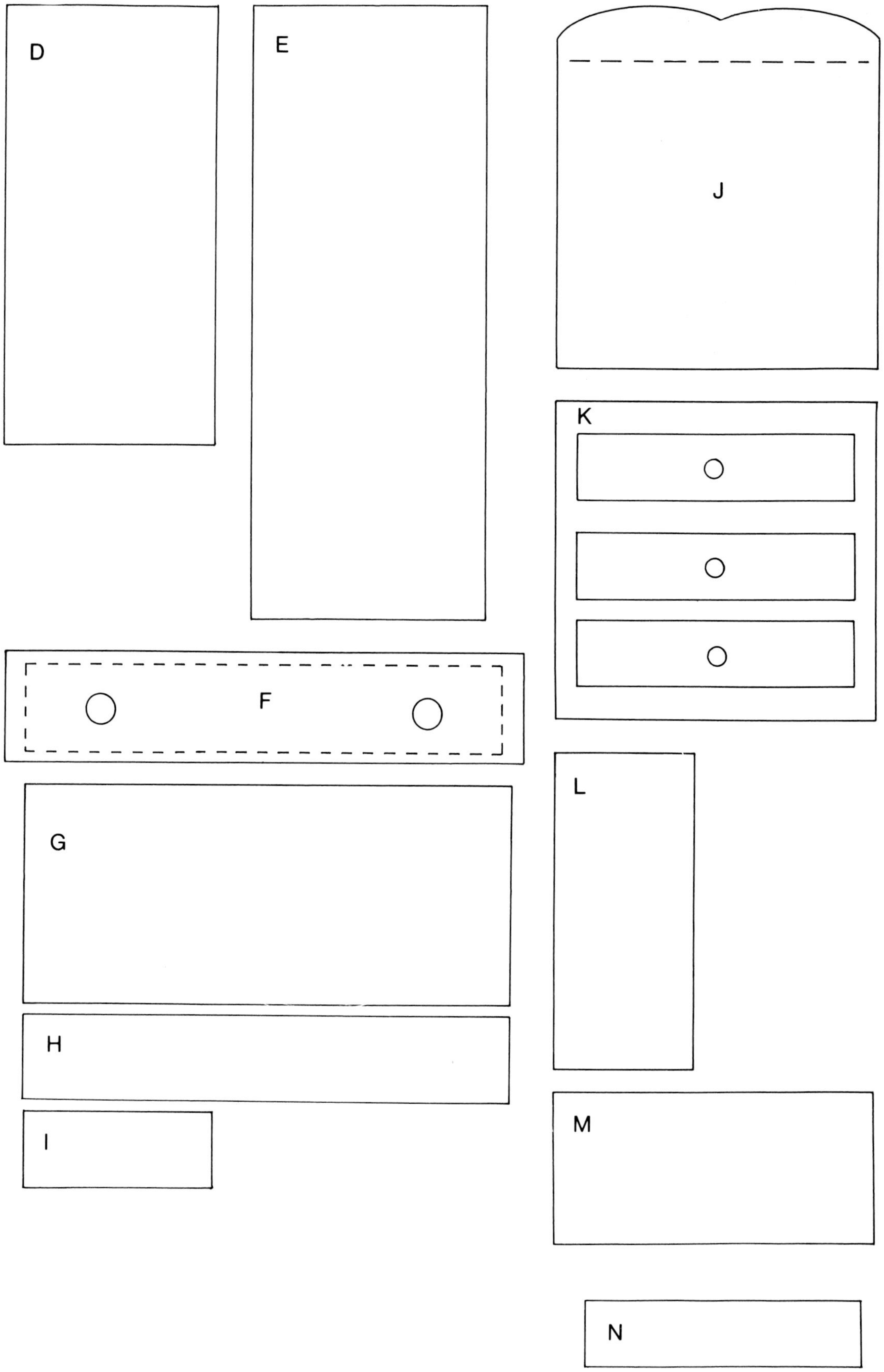

Fig. 106 (continued)
D – side of chest of
drawers (cut out two);
E – top of chest of
drawers; F – front of
drawers (cut out
three); G – base of
drawer; H – back of
drawer; I – side of
drawer (cut out two); J
– back of bedside cabi-
net; K – front of bed-
side cabinet; L – side
of bedside cabinet (cut
out two); M – top of
bedside cabinet; N –
front of bedside cabi-
net drawers (cut out
three)

D

E

J

K

○

○

○

F

○   ○

G

L

H

M

I

N

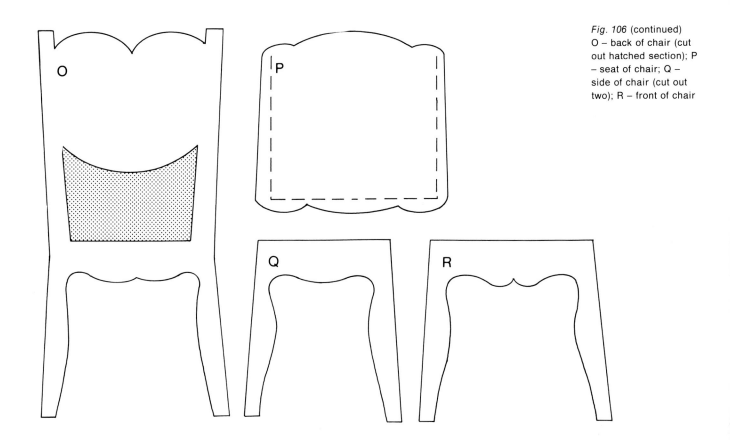

Fig. 106 (continued)
O – back of chair (cut
out hatched section); P
– seat of chair; Q –
side of chair (cut out
two); R – front of chair

Fig. 107
Patterns of picture and key for girl's 21st birth-day cake decorated with a picture in cocoa painting (*plate 89*)

A

B

Fig. 108

150

Fig. 109
Pattern for the oc-
casional cake for a
teenage girl (*plate 93*)

Fig. 110
Pattern for a confir-
mation cake (see *plate 96*)

Fig. 111
Pattern for bell for
multi-purpose cake
(see *plate 97*)

Fig. 112
Pattern for Madonna in
cocoa painting (*plate 99*)

Fig. 113

A

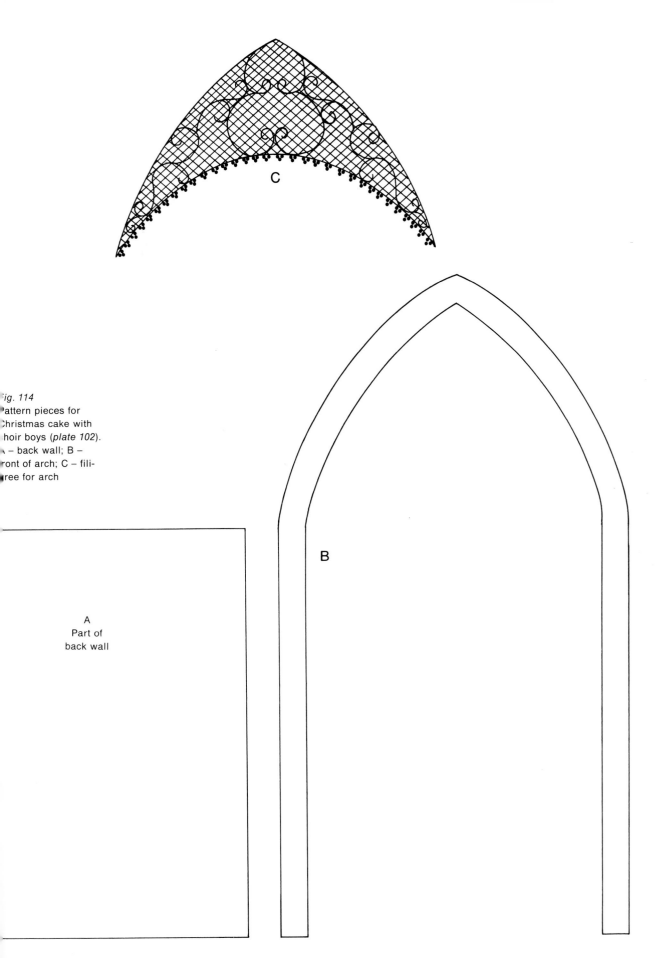

Fig. 114
Pattern pieces for
Christmas cake with
choir boys (*plate 102*).
A – back wall; B –
front of arch; C – fili-
gree for arch

C

B

A
Part of
back wall

D

E

Fig. 114 (continued)
D – right side of arch;
E – left side of arch; F
– side wall; G – front
wall left of arch; H –
left side of roof; I – top
of front step; J – front
of front step; K – side
of front step (cut out
two); L – top of back
step; M – front of back
step; N – side of back
step (cut out two)

F

G

H

I

L

J

K

M

N

Fig. 114 (continued)
O – back/front of sur-
plice (cut out two); P –
sleeve of surplice (cut
out two); Q – ruffle
round neck; R – bow
string (cut out two); S –
bow itself (cut out two);
T – book

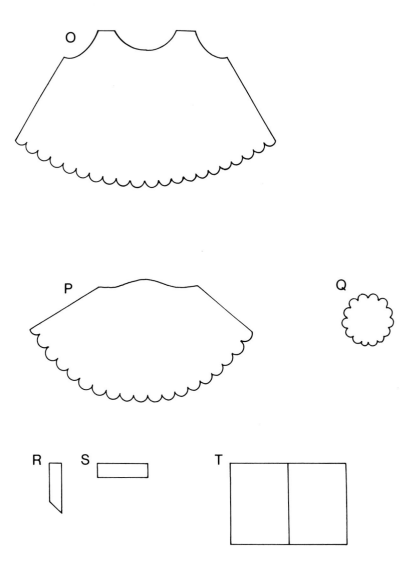

Fig. 115
Note that a mirror im-
age of the wing has to
be traced to make the
second wing

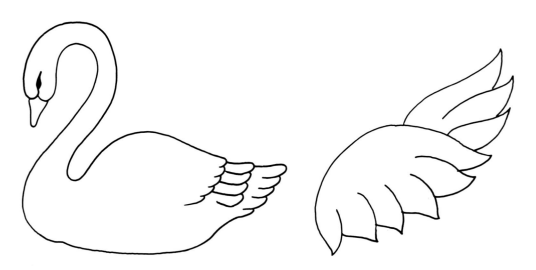

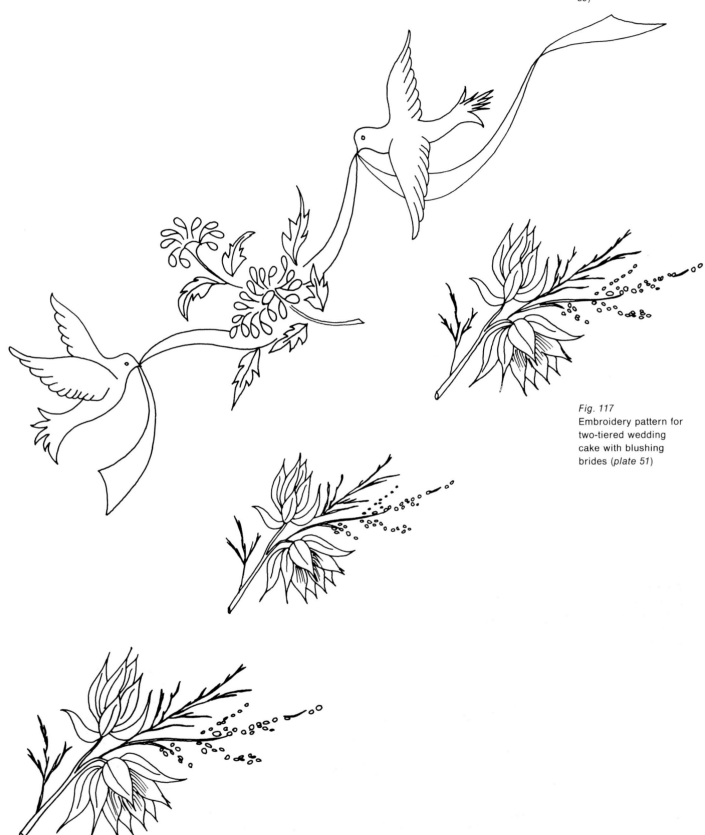

Fig. 116
Embroidery pattern for wedding cake with purple wreath and chrysanthemums (*plate 59*)

Fig. 117
Embroidery pattern for two-tiered wedding cake with blushing brides (*plate 51*)

Fig. 118
Embroidery pattern for
wedding cake with
bride and groom (*plate
65*)

Fig. 119
Embroidery pattern for
the occasional cake for
Mother (*plate 94*)

Fig. 120
Embroidery pattern for
Madonna in cocoa
painting (*plate 99*)

Fig. 121
Embroidery pattern for
cake for a girl's 21st
birthday decorated
with a picture in cocoa
painting (*plate 89*)

Fig. 122
Embroidery pattern for
board of a girl's 21st
birthday decorated
with a picture in cocoa
painting (*plate 89*)

Fig. 123
Embroidery pattern for
fantasy wedding cake
with mice (*plate 66*)

Extra embroidery patterns

Fig. 124

Fig. 125

Fig. 126

Fig. 127

Fig. 128

Fig. 129

Fig. 130

Fig. 131

Fig. 132

Fig. 133

Fig. 134

Fig. 135

Fig. 136

Fig. 137

Fig. 138

Fig. 139

Fig. 140

Fig. 141

Fig. 142

Fig. 143

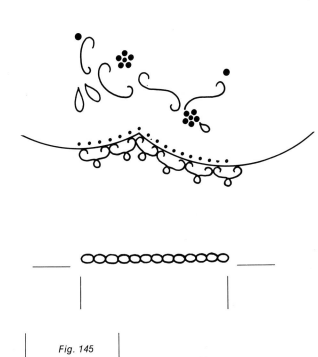

Fig. 144

Fig. 145

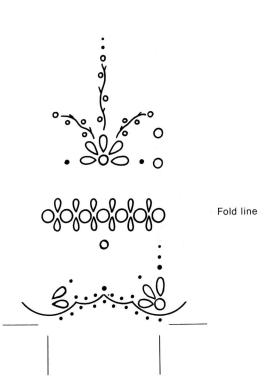

Fold line

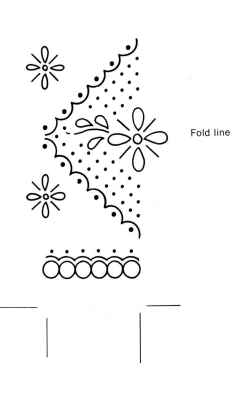

Fold line

Fig. 146
Please note when
making the dots, they
should decrease in
size from the inside to
the outside

Fig. 147

Fig. 148

Fig. 149

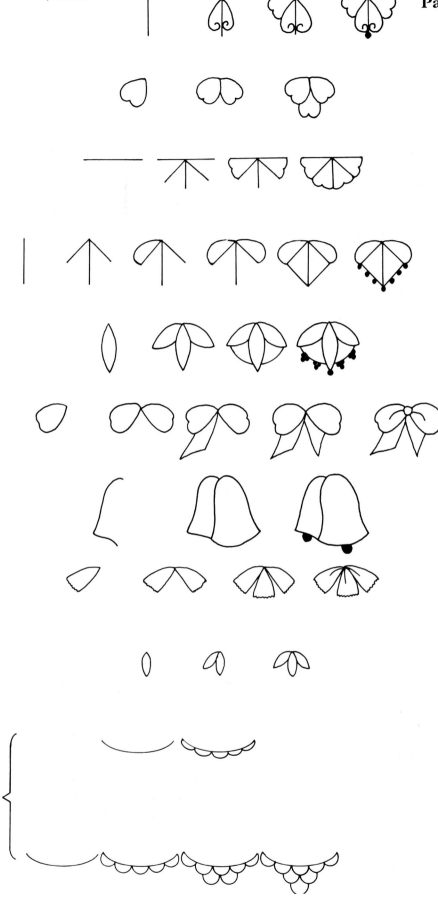

Fig. 150
Shell and lace patterns. A – lace pattern for two-tiered wedding cake with blushing brides (*plate 51*); B – lace pattern for fantasy wedding or anniversary cake with mice (*plate 67*); H – lace pattern for the occasional cake for Mother (*plate 94*); J – lace pattern for wedding cake with purple wreath and chrysanthemums (*plate 59*). The rest of the patterns are extra

Fig. 151

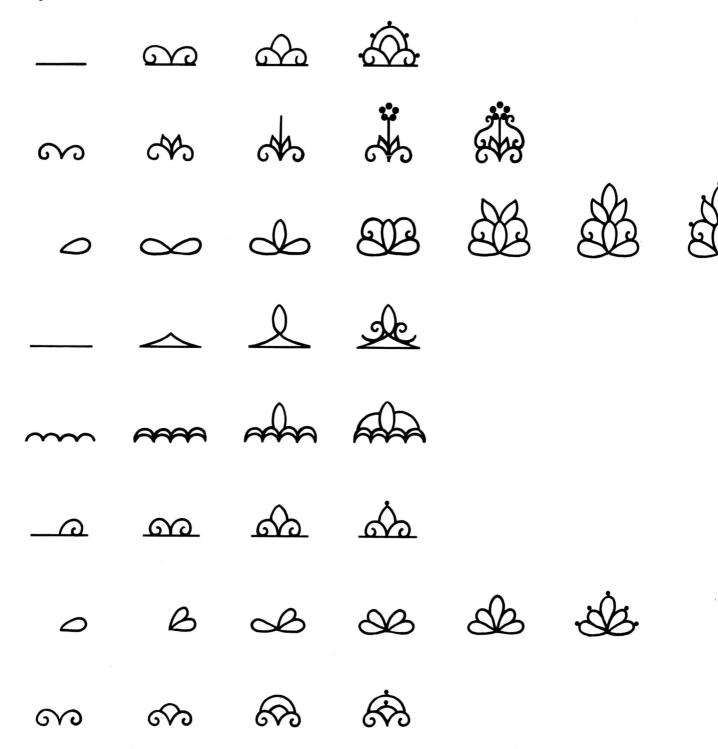

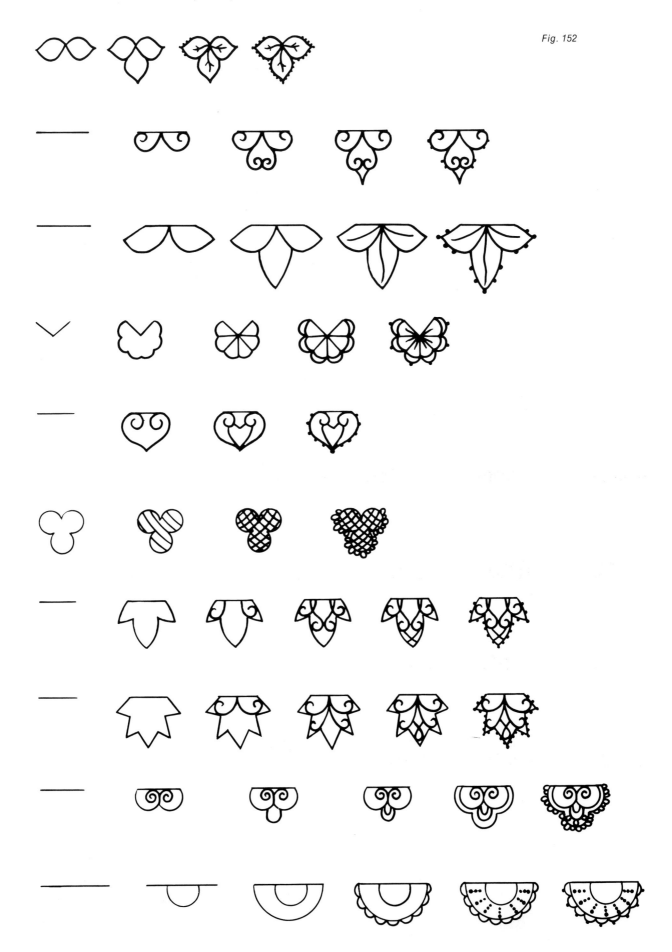

Fig. 152

A B C D E
F G H I J
K L M N O P
Q R S T U
V W X Y Z
1 2 3 4 5
6 7 8 9 0

A B C D E

F G H I J

K L M N O P

Q R S T U

V W X Y Z

1 2 3 4 5

6 7 8 9 0

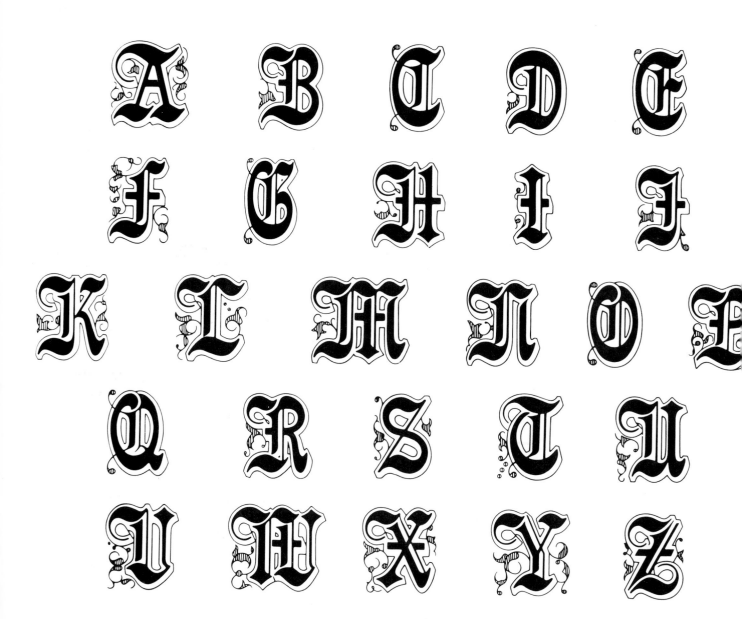

174

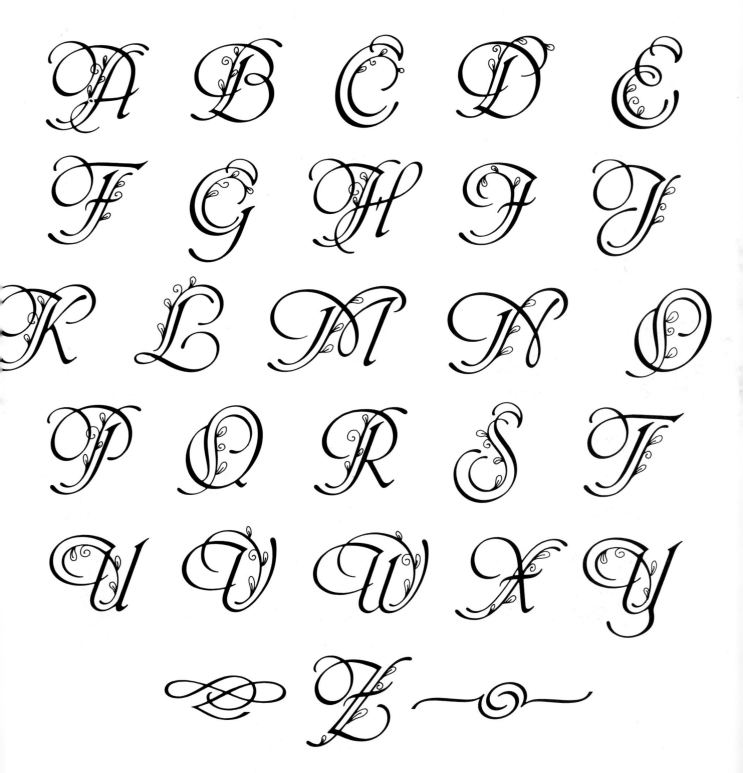

Patterns for cake with pastillage decorations

Fig. 153
Violin: As can be seen in *plates 2 and 31*, black pastillage should be used for pieces, A, B and C, and brown pastillage for piece D. Cut out two scroll shapes to obtain openings and make a horizontal impression in the pastillage between them, in which to slot the bridge (see *fig. 154*). A second solid shape forms the base of the violin box

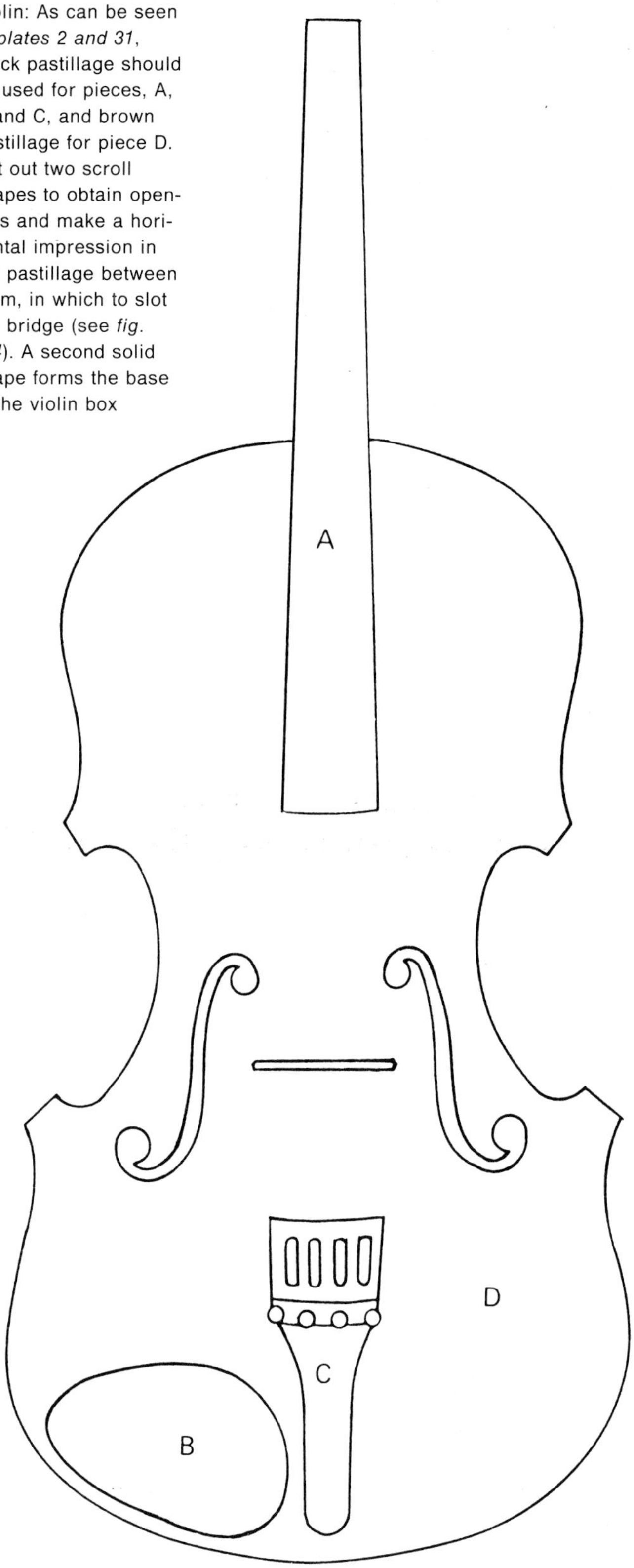

Fig. 154
Bridge of violin (black)

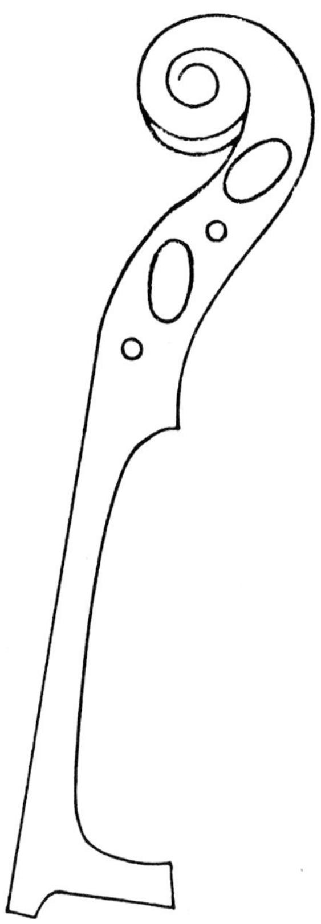

Fig. 155
Neck of violin (brown) to be attached upright to A of *fig. 153*

Fig. 156
Bow of violin